# BERNARD SEAL

# A·M·E·R·I·C·A·N

# VOCABULARY BUILDER 1

**American Vocabulary Builder 1**
Adaptation of Vocabulary Builder 1, by Bernard Seal,
Published by Longman Group Limited, 1987

**Longman, 10 Bank Street, White Plains, N.Y. 10606**

Associated companies:
Longman Group Ltd., London
Longman Cheshire Pty., Melbourne
Longman Paul Pty., Auckland
Copp Clark Pitman, Toronto

Distributed in the United Kingdom by Longman Group
Ltd., Longman House, Burnt Mill, Harlow, Essex CM20
2JE, England and by associated companies, branches,
and representatives throughout the world.

ISBN: 0-8013-0496-2

8 9 10-CRS-99 98 97 96 95 94

# Contents

# Introduction

## To the student

This book is intended to help you expand your vocabulary. It is written for students who are approaching the intermediate level. While studying *American Vocabulary Builder 1*, it is a good idea for you to use a dictionary for intermediate learners in English, such as the *Longman Dictionary of American English.*

*American Vocabulary Builder 1* is divided into three sections: **The human body, The inner self**, and **The world around us**. Each section has ten units that deal with different groups of words, and each unit contains several parts.

The first part is called **Words in context** and contains a passage or passages for you to read and study. You should try to read these passages without a dictionary. The key words are in dark print and in most cases you should be able to guess the meaning of these words from the way they are used in the passage. If you are not sure of the meaning of a word, always look back at the sentence before and after it. These sentences will often help to explain the word. You will also have a general idea of the meaning, because all the key words are closely related. For example, the first unit is called **Age**, and all the key words (old, elderly, middle-aged, adult, child, baby, etc.) are connected in some way with describing someone's age. This should help you guess the meaning of the words that you don't know.

**Exercise 1** follows the **Words in context** passage. This is a reading comprehension exercise. In many cases the questions focus on the meanings of the key words.

**Exercise 2** and **Exercise 3** test your knowledge of the key words in the passage. Before you do these exercises you should always look back at the passage and see how the key words have been used.

Each unit also has a fourth exercise called either **Dictionary work** or **Just for fun**. The **Dictionary work** exercise introduces more vocabulary related to the subject of the unit. You will usually need a dictionary for this exercise because you do not have a passage to help you guess the meaning of the words. The **Just for fun** exercises give you a chance to have some fun with the words you have been studying.

The final section, **Think about**, should help you to use the words in an interesting discussion.

At the end of each five units, you can review the words you have studied in the **Vocabulary review** section. Your knowledge of these words is tested in one of the six **Test yourself** exercises.

There is also an **Index** of key words at the back of the book, which includes a phonetic guide to pronunciation. The **Index** gives the number of each unit in which the word appears.

## To the teacher

*American Vocabulary Builders* can be used either as classroom material or as self-study material for high-beginning to intermediate students who want to build their vocabulary.

### The approach

*American Vocabulary Builders* present key words in lexical sets embedded in texts. The meanings of the items can often be guessed from their context, and knowledge of the words is then extended, practiced, and tested in a series of exercises.

Each book is divided into three large subject areas, containing ten units. Each unit teaches a lexical set, such as verbs describing different ways of moving, adjectives describing different degrees of happiness and sadness, types of buildings  or types of animals. There are two principal reasons for teaching vocabulary in sets. First, students often feel that they learn vocabulary in a somewhat random way. Putting the words into lexical sets makes their study more structured. Each unit studied gives them a sense of measurable progress. Secondly, since all the words in a lexical set are related, the student has an immediate clue as to the meaning of a previously unknown word. Thus, for example, when encountering the word "terrified" in the unit on fear, the student will realize that it has something to do with being afraid.

Each lexical set is presented in a reading passage or passages at the beginning of a unit. These passages may seem difficult. The syntax and structures in them have not been tightly controlled and you may well feel that the language is beyond the productive capabilities of your students. This has been done intentionally. The aim is to have students reading at a level that stretches and challenges them, provided that they are able to maintain a general sense of what the text is about.

The passages have been carefully written so that the more difficult lexical items can be guessed from the context in which they occur. This may often involve a degree of textual redundancy which enables the meaning of the target items to be made clearer by the extra clues. Given these clues, the students learn to guess the meanings of words from their context and are encouraged not to become too dependent on the dictionary while they are reading. It is important that students develop good reading habits. They should learn to read fluently, tolerating a certain degree of ambiguity while maintaining an interest in the gist of the passage.

The target words are clearly marked in a bold typeface on their first occurrence in the text. Each target item occurs again in at least one of the exercises that follow. These exercises are designed to reinforce the meanings of the target words and to test the students' understanding of how they should be used. The fact that each target item appears in bold print enables the student to return to the original **Words in context** passage to find an example of its usage. This will help them do the exercises.

### Contents of a unit

● *Words in context*
A short passage or passages containing the target words in the lexical set.

● *Exercise 1*
A comprehension exercise which leads students to understand the overall meaning of the passage and at the same time focuses attention on some of the key vocabulary items.

● *Exercises 2 and 3*
Each of the target lexical items is encountered in at least one of these exercises. The exercises are designed to extend the students' understanding of the items.

● *Dictionary work/Just for fun*
**Dictionary work** exercises encourage students to expand their vocabulary by introducing a lexical set related to the topic of the unit. The students will usually need a dictionary to complete these exercises.

**Just for fun** exercises may take various forms: ranking and rating exercises, games, and other communicative activities. These exercises are intended to further the students' interest in the topic and to give them an opportunity to use some of the target lexical items in a stress-free context.

● *Think about*
These are discussion questions, designed to activate the students' production of the target words in a conversation or discussion.

### How to use American Vocabulary Builders in the classroom
Each unit is designed so that it can form the basis of a one-hour lesson. However, the material should be flexible enough to be used in parts over a series of lessons if preferred. Teachers may also find that they can use the book to combine in-class work with homework.

One of the main aims of the *American Vocabulary Builders* is to promote a problem-solving approach to vocabulary learning. On their first encounter with the target items in the reading passages, students are expected to try to work out meanings without much teacher guidance and without the use of a dictionary. Be aware, therefore, that too much pre-teaching will destroy the point of the exercises. It is suggested that you introduce the topic of the unit with some brief pre-questions relating to the topic. Then, if you want to pre-teach some vocabulary items, only pre-teach those words that you feel will facilitate your students' understanding of the text, but which are not key words, i.e., words which do not appear in bold print in the text.

The first time you use the book, you should explain to the students why you do not want them to use a dictionary when studying the passages. Point out how many of the difficult words can be guessed from their context. This can be illustrated by taking one of the passages and going through it with the class. The students will soon get used to searching for the context clues and doing without a dictionary.

Let your students work silently once they start reading the passage. When they are ready they should attempt to answer the questions in **Exercise 1**. Encourage students to share their answers in pairs.

At this stage (when all students have read the passage and attempted **Exercise 1**) you may want to read the passage aloud so that they can hear how the words are pronounced. Your phrasing may also help the students to understand the passage better. It is best if you wait until they have read through the passage silently before they hear it, because this promotes the habit of silent reading when they are on their own.

**Exercise 2** and **Exercise 3** may then be done either as whole class or pair work activities, or individually, whichever seems more appropriate. In general, easier exercises should be done individually, with the students checking their answers with their neighbors, and more difficult problem-solving exercises should be done in pairs or small groups.

**Just for fun** exercises are designed for work in pairs or small groups. Make sure the students are absolutely clear about what they have to do in their groups. This should be a relaxed, active and enjoyable phase of the lesson.

**Dictionary work** exercises may either be done in class with dictionaries or set as homework.

The **Think about** questions are intended to get students talking and using the vocabulary of the lesson. There are only a few discussion questions in each unit, so you may wish to add some of your own.

It is possible to teach the units in any order. They have not been sequenced in difficulty and do not rely on the students having studied one unit in order to study the next. However, in order to use the **Test yourself** sections effectively, it is best to teach the units in groups of five, i.e., Units 1.1 to 1.5 or 2.6 to 2.10.

## *Acknowledgments*

Inevitably, when a textbook takes a very long time to go from an idea to a final product, there are many people who contribute along the way. The idea for this book started at least five years ago. The texts and exercises have gone through many stages and revisions before reaching the final layout and texts in this book. Family, friends, and colleagues have contributed in many different ways. Some have contributed ideas, suggested changes and tested materials. Some have done typing and provided office space and facilities. Others have encouraged and motivated. To all of you, I give many thanks.

Some special thanks are due to the following for their help: Mary Alvin, Carole Brown, Dave Brown, Kelly Davis, Dr. Ian Dunlop, Sue Maingay, Robert O'Neill, Della Summers, Linda Ward, and Norma Williams. And to my wife, Chris.

# 1 The human body

## 1.1 Age

"How old are you?" It's a simple question, and there is usually a simple answer: "sixteen years old," "twenty years old," "fifty-five," etc. But if someone is described as young or middle-aged or old, then how old is that person? It's difficult to know because these are words that have different meanings for different people.

Except for the word teenager, which describes someone whose age ends in the syllable "teen" (such as fourteen, fifteen or sixteen), words which describe age are not exact. When, for example, does a baby stop being called a baby and become a young child? When does a boy become a young man and a little girl become a young woman? At what age does middle age begin? When do you call someone elderly and not simply old? At what age does someone become an adult? In some countries, it is when the government says a person is old enough to vote. Is that really the difference between a child and an adult?

The answers to these questions partly depend on how old you are. There is a saying that old age is always ten years older than yourself. If you are fifteen, then you think someone of twenty-five is old. At thirty, forty seems old. If you are seventy, then you probably think someone of eighty is old. A recent survey showed that there was some truth in the old saying. People were asked, "When is middle age?" Those in their early twenties usually answered, "Between thirty-five and fifty," and people in their thirties answered, "Between forty-five and sixty."

**Words in context**
*Read the following passage and do the exercises.*

## Exercise 1

*Decide whether these statements are true (T) or false (F) according to the passage.*

1 _____ When people are asked their age, they usually answer with a number.

2 _____ If someone tells you that he or she is middle-aged, you know the exact age of that person.

3 _____ It is possible to call someone who is twelve a teenager.

4 _____ There is an exact age when a baby becomes a young child.

5 _____ "Elderly" is similar in meaning to "old."

6 _____ Some governments say that an adult is a person who can vote.

7 _____ According to the saying, if you are twenty-nine, then you think someone of thirty is old.

8 _____ As you get older, your ideas change about when middle age begins.

## Exercise 2

*Match each sentence in column A with a sentence in column B which has almost the same meaning.*

| A | B |
|---|---|
| 1 _____ He is a five-year-old boy. | a) He's still a baby. |
| 2 _____ She is between the ages of thirty and forty. | b) He's in his twenties. |
| 3 _____ He is fifteen. | c) She's a teenager. |
| 4 _____ She is eight years old. | d) She's middle-aged. |
| 5 _____ She is over seventy years old. | e) She's in her thirties. |
| 6 _____ He is twelve months old. | f) He's a teenager. |
| 7 _____ She is fifty-four years old. | g) He's a child. |
| 8 _____ She is between the ages of thirteen and nineteen. | h) She's an elderly lady. |
| 9 _____ He is either twenty-four or twenty-five. | i) She's a little girl. |

## Just for fun

*When does a baby become a child? When does a child become a young man or woman?*
*Fill in the chart and compare your answers with other people's.*

| | age | | |
|---|---|---|---|
| a baby | from __0__ years | to _____ years | |
| a child | from _____ years | to _____ years | |
| a young man/woman | from _____ years | to _____ years | |
| a middle-aged man/woman | from _____ years | to _____ years | |
| an old man/woman | from _____ years | to the end of your life | |

## Think about

1  How would you describe yourself: young, old, middle-aged, a boy, a man, a girl, a woman?

2  When is someone considered to be an adult in your country?

3  What are the signs of aging?

4  How important is age? In marriage? In work?

# 1.2 Beauty

**Words in context**  *Read the following passage and do the exercises.*

How important is your appearance? Although everyone wants to be **good-looking**, are **beautiful** people always happier people? For example, it must be a problem to be a really beautiful woman, because some men may be more interested in looking at you than talking to you. They think of you as a picture rather than a person. There are also some people who think that women who are exceptionally **pretty** and men who are particularly **handsome** must be stupid. They believe that only **unattractive** people can be intelligent.

On the other hand, no one wants to be really **ugly**, and have a face that even your mother doesn't want to look at; and no one wants to be **plain** either – that is, to be neither attractive nor unattractive, and have a face that is easily forgotten.

Being **attractive** is like being rich – it can help you find happiness, but it doesn't always make you happy. So maybe the best thing is not to worry too much about how you look, but simply try to be an interesting person. For interesting people have interesting faces, and interesting faces are almost always attractive.

## Exercise 1

*Decide whether these statements are true (T), false (F), or impossible to know (IK) according to the passage.*

1 _____ Everyone wants to be attractive.

2 _____ Most beautiful people are unhappy.

3 _____ No one likes to talk to a very pretty woman.

4 _____ Some people think that handsome men are unintelligent.

5 _____ Attractive men and women are usually intelligent.

6 _____ Ugly people are not happy people.

7 _____ A plain face is easily forgotten.

8 _____ Not many interesting people are also attractive.

## Exercise 2

*Put these words in order from most negative (worst to look at) to most positive (best to look at).*

| a) very attractive | b) very ugly | c) very beautiful | d) plain | e) quite good-looking | f) unattractive |

1 _____     2 _____     3 _____     4 _____     5 _____     6 _____

## Exercise 3

*Some of the words which describe attractiveness are mostly used to describe males and others to describe females. Look at the examples next to the chart. Then fill in the chart by putting an X in the right boxes.*

| | male ♂ | female ♀ | either ♂♀ |
|---|---|---|---|
| attractive | | | X |
| beautiful | | | |
| good-looking | | | |
| handsome | | | |
| pretty | | | |
| ugly | | | |

a good-looking man
an attractive girl
a handsome man
an ugly woman
a beautiful lady
a pretty girl
a beautiful woman
an ugly man
a pretty woman
an attractive man
a good-looking woman
a handsome man

## Dictionary work

*Put a (+) sign next to the "attractive" positive words and a (−) next to the "unattractive" negative words. Do as many as you can and then check your answers in a dictionary.*

1 _____ awful      2 _____ wonderful      3 _____ horrible      4 _____ lovely

5 _____ great      6 _____ nice      7 _____ pleasant      8 _____ revolting

9 _____ elegant      10 _____ nasty      11 _____ hideous      12 _____ gorgeous

13 _____ terrible      14 _____ ghastly      15 _____ marvelous      16 _____ ugly

## Think about

1 Who is the most beautiful woman and the best-looking man in the world?
(Think about famous people such as movie stars and rock stars.)

2 Do you think it's difficult to be very good-looking? Why? Why not?

3 How important is it to look attractive? Why?

4 Look at these common English expressions and then decide whether you agree with them.

a) Beauty is only skin deep.
b) Your face is your fortune.
c) Beauty is in the eye of the beholder (i.e., the person who is looking).

# 1.3 Parts of the face

**Words in context**   *Read the following passages and do the exercises.*

People who cannot hear often learn to understand a spoken language not with their **ears** but with their **eyes**. They watch the **mouth** of the person talking and follow the movement of his or her **lips**. This is called lip-reading. (Now answer question 1, Exercise 1.)

One of the most difficult sounds for a foreign student to make in English is the "th" sound, as in the word "**tooth**." To make this sound, you put the tip of the **tongue** under your top teeth. Then you push the tongue up a little and the air comes out at the sides of the mouth. (Now answer question 2.)

Some people think that the distance between your hair and your **eyebrows** is a sign of how intelligent you are. The bigger your **forehead** is, the more intelligent you are supposed to be. (Now answer question 3.)

Nowadays, if you don't like your **nose**, you can have it changed with plastic surgery. Plastic surgeons can change your face in many other ways too. They can make your **cheeks** a little rounder or higher under the eyes. If you don't like your **chin**, a plastic surgeon can break your **jaw** and remake the whole lower half of your face. If you think your **skin** looks too old and full of **wrinkles**, they can take the wrinkles away and make you look twenty years younger. (Now answer question 4.)

Women often disagree about men having **beards** and **mustaches**. Some women think that hair on a man's chin makes him look friendly and attractive. Other women think beards *look* all right but they don't like to touch them. As for mustaches, there are some women who think they are very attractive, and others who think that a mustache makes a man look cold and mean. (Now answer question 5.)

Usually, only women wear make-up. They are lucky. They can put a little black mascara on their **eyelashes** and some eyeshadow on their **eyelids**, and look fresh and attractive, even when they are really tired. But the morning after a very late night, a man just has to look terrible! (Now answer question 6.)

## Exercise 1

*Choose the best answer according to the information in the passages.*

1 People who cannot hear usually watch a speaker's
   a) lips   b) eyes   c) ears

2 You make the "th" sound in English by having
   a) the top teeth under the tongue
   b) the top teeth above the tongue
   c) the tongue above the top teeth

3 Intelligent people are said to have big
   a) eyebrows   b) foreheads   c) heads

4 A plastic surgeon may break the jawbone to change the shape of a person's
   a) cheeks   b) wrinkles   c) chin

5 A mustache is hair on the
   a) upper lip   b) chin   c) head

6 Most men don't
   a) have eyelashes   b) wear eyeshadow
   c) have eyelids

## Exercise 2

*Name the parts of the face in the pictures.*

| forehead | eyebrow | cheek | lips | mustache | chin | tongue | tooth | ear | eyelashes |

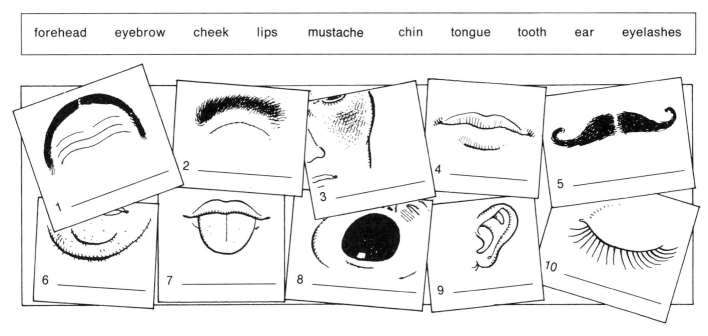

## Exercise 3

*Answer these questions with the parts of the face given below.*

| a) nose | b) teeth | c) ears | d) eyebrows | e) eyelids | f) beard |

1 You hear with them. _____

2 You raise them when you are surprised. _____

3 A man grows it to cover his chin. _____

4 You close them when you go to sleep. _____

5 You can buy false ones to help you bite. _____

6 You smell with it. _____

## Just for fun

*Which part of the face is different from the other three in each group and why?*
*More than one answer may be possible. Compare your answers with other people's.*

| | | | |
|---|---|---|---|
| 1 eyes | teeth | tongue | lips |
| 2 mustache | nose | eyelash | eyebrow |
| 3 jaw | chin | eyelid | beard |
| 4 mouth | cheeks | ears | eyebrows |
| 5 ears | nose | forehead | eyes |
| 6 skin | wrinkle | tooth | cheek |

## Think about

1 Describe the face of someone you know well.
2 Would you ever have plastic surgery? Why? Why not?
3 Do you like beards and mustaches? Why do you think men grow them?
4 The "th" sound is a difficult sound in English. Which sounds are difficult for foreigners to make in your language? Can you explain how to make them?

# 1.4 Hair

JILL: You know, Lisa, I love your **hair**. It's so **thick** and **dark** and **curly**. Are those curls natural or did you get your hair **permed**?

LISA: Are you kidding? I can't afford a perm. This is all natural. But I'll tell you something funny. As a kid, I hated curly hair. I always wanted to have **straight** hair, or **wavy** hair like yours. And I always wished I were **blond**, like you.

JILL: Really? You must be crazy. Your hair's great. I wish my hair weren't so **light**, and I wish it were curlier. And your hair is so thick and mine's so **thin**. Oh dear, I just never know what to do with my hair. Should I have it cut really **short**, or should I have it **medium length**? Or do you like it **long** like this?

LISA: How about a **punk** haircut? You could have it very short at the sides and long at the back and on top, and then you could put some red, blue and **green** in it.

JILL: Very funny. But you're right about one thing, Lisa, I really should dye my hair. Do you know I have a few **gray** hairs already and I'm only twenty-six.

LISA: Well, at least we women don't have to worry about going **bald**. There's baldness in my family, you know. My father hasn't got a hair on his head. He went bald at thirty.

JILL: Hm, I don't know. Maybe I'd look nice bald . . . what do you think?

## Exercise 1

*Decide whether these statements are true (T) or false (F) according to the dialogue.*

1 _____ Jill likes curly hair.

2 _____ Lisa's hair is curly.

3 _____ Lisa has a perm.

4 _____ Jill has wavy hair.

5 _____ Jill has thick hair.

6 _____ Jill has long hair.

7 _____ Jill thinks she would look nice with a punk haircut.

8 _____ Jill has twenty-six gray hairs.

9 _____ Jill wants to change the color of her hair.

10 _____ Lisa's father is bald.

# Exercise 2

Match these different types of hair and hairstyle with the pictures.

a) bald     b) punk     c) permed     d) dark hair     e) light hair     f) straight hair

1 _____     2 _____     3 _____     4 _____     5 _____     6 _____

# Exercise 3

Decide whether these words describe hair color, hair length, hair quantity or hair type.
Then write them in the appropriate columns.

| blond | thick | medium length | curly | short | wavy | gray | thin |

| color | length | quantity | type |
|-------|--------|----------|------|
| _____ | _____ | _____ | _____ |
| _____ | _____ | _____ | _____ |

# Dictionary work

The verbs in column A describe things we do to our hair. The words in column B are
the things we use to do them. Match each verb in column A with a word in column B
and then check your answers in a dictionary.

|  | **A** |  | **B** |
|---|-------|---|-------|
| 1 _____ | cut it | a) | a towel |
| 2 _____ | wash it | b) | a razor |
|  | with |  |  |
| 3 _____ | shave it off | c) | shampoo |
| 4 _____ | dry it | d) | scissors |

# Think about

1 What kind of hairstyle do you have now? Can you describe the different hairstyles
  you have had in the past?
2 Which hairstyles can you suggest for your classmates and friends?
3 Which hairstyles are fashionable at the moment?
4 "Hairstyle is a very important way for people to say something about who they are
  and what they believe." Do you agree with this statement? Why? Why not?

# 1.5 Seeing and sight

**Words in context** *Read the following passages and do the exercises.*

The teacher **glared at** the two students sitting at the back of the class. She was very angry and shouted at them, "Hey, you two. Stop that immediately or I'll give you extra work to do after class." (Now answer question 1, Exercise 1.)

The farmer's wife heard a noise outside. She went to the front door and opened it. "Is that you out there, Jack?" she asked, **peering** into the darkness. (Now answer question 4.)

Sarah **gazed** out of the window. The streets were crowded with people who were busy doing their Christmas shopping, but Sarah was not really **looking at** them. She was thinking about Tom and where he was. (Now answer question 6.)

The two spies talked on the telephone for the last time. "Boris, you are not to speak to me at the embassy party, but you must watch my face carefully. I will **wink** at you. If I close my right eye, you are to kill the man, but if I wink with my left eye, you are to kill the woman. Understand?" (Now answer question 2.)

The camera flash went off and the girl **blinked**. "I'm sorry. You'd better take another photograph. I think I blinked and I'm sure you don't want a picture of me with my eyes closed, do you?" (Now answer question 7.)

The bookseller picked up the book and **examined** it for several minutes. Finally he looked up at the woman and said, "OK, I'll give you twenty dollars for it." (Now answer question 3.)

"Johnny, why are you **staring at** that lady?"
"I think she's a famous movie star."
"It doesn't matter who she is. It's not polite to stare like that." (Now answer question 5.)

Detective Chang held a photograph in his hand. "Well," he said, "was this the man you saw?" "I'm not sure," said the young man. "I only **glanced at** him for a second." (Now answer question 8.)

## Exercise 1

*Choose the best answer according to the passages.*

1 The teacher looked at the students
   a) for a long time   b) quickly   c) angrily

2 Boris will kill the man if the spy closes
   a) his left eye   b) his right eye   c) both eyes

3 The bookseller looked at the book
   a) very carefully   b) very quickly   c) with difficulty

4 The farmer's wife looked outside
   a) nervously   b) with difficulty   c) quickly

5 Johnny looked at the lady
   a) for a long time   b) quickly   c) angrily

6 Sarah was looking carefully at
   a) the people   b) Tom   c) no one

7 The girl blinked because
   a) the light flashed   b) her eyes were closed
   c) she was thinking

8 The young man was not sure who the man in the photograph was because
   a) it was dark when he saw him
   b) the photograph was not clear
   c) he had not looked at him carefully

16

## Exercise 2

*Match each of these verbs with its meaning. Put an X in the right box, as in the example.*

|  | blink | glare | examine | glance | stare | peer | wink | gaze |
|---|---|---|---|---|---|---|---|---|
| to look quickly |  |  |  | X |  |  |  |  |
| to close and open one eye quickly |  |  |  |  |  |  |  |  |
| to look at closely |  |  |  |  |  |  |  |  |
| to look steadily (often feeling thoughtful) |  |  |  |  |  |  |  |  |
| to look hard and unpleasantly |  |  |  |  |  |  |  |  |
| to look with difficulty |  |  |  |  |  |  |  |  |
| to close and open both eyes quickly |  |  |  |  |  |  |  |  |
| to look steadily for a long time |  |  |  |  |  |  |  |  |

## Dictionary work

*Match the first half of the sentence in column A with the second half in column B. More than one answer is sometimes possible, but there is always one best answer. Do as many as you can. Then check any words you don't know in a dictionary and finish the exercise.*

**A**

1 _____ If you can't see anything at all,

2 _____ If you want to look closely at the moon,

3 _____ If strong light hurts your eyes,

4 _____ If you have perfect eyesight,

5 _____ If you have difficulty seeing things across a room,

6 _____ If you want to watch birds in the countryside,

7 _____ If you need glasses but don't like wearing them,

**B**

a) you don't need glasses.

b) you need a pair of binoculars.

c) you should wear contact lenses.

d) you are nearsighted.

e) you need a telescope.

f) you are blind.

g) you should wear sunglasses.

## Think about

1 When and why do people stare?
2 What does a wink mean in your country?
3 Do you have to wear glasses? What sort of eyesight do you have?
4 Are glasses and contact lenses expensive in your country?

# Vocabulary review

## 1 The human body (Units 1.1–1.5)

### 1.1 Age

adult
baby
boy
child
elderly
girl
in one's twenties
little
little boy/girl
man
middle age
middle-aged
old
old age
teenager
woman
years old
young
young man/woman/child

### 1.2 Beauty

attractive
awful
beautiful
elegant
ghastly
good-looking
gorgeous
great
handsome
hideous
horrible
lovely
marvelous
nasty
nice
plain
pleasant
pretty
revolting
terrible
ugly
unattractive
wonderful

### 1.3 Parts of the face

beard
cheek
chin
ear
eye
eyebrow
eyelash
eyelid
forehead
jaw
lip
mustache
mouth
nose
skin
tongue
tooth
wrinkle

### 1.4 Hair

bald
blond
curly
cut
dark
dry
gray
hair
light
long
medium length
permed
punk
razor
scissors
shampoo
shave
short
straight
thick
thin
towel
wash
wavy

### 1.5 Seeing and sight

binoculars
blind
blink
contact lenses
examine
eyesight
gaze
glance at
glare at
glasses
look at
peer
perfect eye sight
near sighted
stare at
sunglasses
telescope
wink

# Test yourself 1

Use the words from the **Vocabulary review** to help you fill the blanks in these sentences.
In some cases you have been given the last letter of the word. More than one answer may be
possible, but there is usually one best answer.

1 It is true that my grandmother is an _____y lady, but she is still very

2 _____t. She always dresses beautifully.

3 "Why are you _____g at those people over there?"

4 "I'm just surprised to see a _____ _____ couple dancing like that."

5 My eyes are killing me. I think one of my _____ has fallen into my eye.

6 Is he naturally _____ or did he shave his head?

7 My girlfriend has asked me to shave off my _____d. She says it feels funny against

8 her _____k when we kiss.

9 I always thought I looked _____y in glasses, so I decided to buy myself some

10 _____ _____, even though they are much more expensive.

11 Of course she can't walk yet, she is still only a _____.

12 How often do you _____h your hair?

13 He's so tall he banged his _____ against the top of the door, and now he has a cut

14 above his left _____w.

15 All the girls think he's so _____e. They think he should become a movie star.

16 Coming in from the rain, she went into the bathroom and _____ her long,

17 _____k hair.

18 Pass me the _____. I want to get a better look at that football player.

19 Doctor, please _____e my son. I think his leg is broken.

"How old is your daughter?"

20 "She's still a _____, but she'll be twenty next year."

21 Could you quickly _____e at my homework and tell me how many I got right?

22 This is my favorite picture. I think it's really _____y.

23 The bus fare is eighty cents for _____ and forty cents for children.

24 I think his hair is _____s. It is so wonderfully

25 _____y.

# 1.6 Body size and body parts

**Words in context**   *Read the following passage and do the exercises.*

Mr. and Mrs. Smith were a very **average** couple. His name was John. Her name was Mary. They lived in an average-sized house and had two average children — one boy and one girl.

Were they **tall**? Mr. and Mrs. Smith were neither tall nor **short**. They were both **average height**. He was average height for a man and she was average height for a woman.

Were they **fat**? Mr. Smith was certainly not **weak** or **skinny**, but he was not **strong** or **well-built** either. He was just medium build and his **shoulders** and **chest** were neither very **broad** nor very **narrow**. His wife, too, could never be described as **thin** or **slim**, but then again, she was not **overweight** or fat either. Her **waist** was neither too **big** nor too narrow. It was just . . . average size.

It was very easy for Mr. and Mrs. Smith to buy clothes because every part of their bodies was average size too. Their **feet** were neither very big not very **small**. Their **hips** were not too wide. And their legs were neither too short not too long.

Yes, the Smiths were a very average couple. Except for one thing. They were the only couple in the country who were average in so many different ways at the same time. The Smiths were in fact . . . unique.

## Exercise 1

*Decide whether the following statements are true (T) or false (F) according to the passage.*

1 _____   Mr. and Mrs. Smith had two children named John and Mary.

2 _____   Mr. Smith was at least six feet six.

3 _____   Mrs. Smith was average height.

4 _____   Mr. Smith was a skinny man.

5 _____   Mrs. Smith probably weighed about 160 pounds.

6 _____   Mrs. Smith had a very small waist.

7 _____   Mr. Smith had average-sized feet.

8 _____   The Smiths were completely average.

## Exercise 2

Which sentences describe Alan (A) and which describe Bob (B)?

1 _____ He has broad shoulders.

2 _____ He looks very strong.

3 _____ He's very tall.

4 _____ He's rather short.

5 _____ He has a narrow waist.

6 _____ He's a little overweight.

7 _____ He looks very weak.

Alan

Bob

## Exercise 3

Put these adjectives in order from smallest (1) to biggest (5).

| a) skinny | b) fat | c) slim | d) overweight | e) well-built |

1 _____ (unattractively thin)　　2 _____ (attractively thin)　　3 _____ (good muscles)

4 _____ (needs to go on a diet)　　5 _____ (unattractively big)

## Dictionary work

Which of these parts are inside the body and which are outside? Write (I) next to those which are inside and (O) next to those which are outside. Do as many as you can and then check your answers in a dictionary.

1 _____ heart　　　2 _____ chest　　　3 _____ neck　　　4 _____ intestines

5 _____ shoulders　6 _____ skin　　　7 _____ liver　　　8 _____ blood

9 _____ muscle　　10 _____ bone　　11 _____ buttocks　12 _____ hips

13 _____ brain　　14 _____ lungs　　15 _____ back　　　16 _____ feet

## Think about

1 What is the average height for men and women in your country? Is it changing?
2 What are the advantages and disadvantages of being either very tall or very short?
3 Can you think of some good ways of keeping these parts of the body in good condition: heart, lungs, skin, bone, muscle?
4 Describe some ways of losing weight.

# 1.7 Arms and hands

**Words in context**   Read the following passage and do the exercises.

The **arms** and **hands** of our prehistoric ancestors were probably not very different from the human arm and hand today. The upper and lower joints of the arm, **elbow** and **wrist**, were probably very similar, and the basic structure of the hand with its five **fingers** was also the same. But according to some scientists, there has been an important change – a change in the way we hold things.

Many hundreds of thousands of years ago, our ancestors could hold things in only one way. This is called the power grip. The power grip is used, for example, to hold a hammer or a piece of wood. With this grip, you hold the object in the **palm** of the hand with four fingers on one side and the **thumb** on the other.

Later, the human hand developed a second grip, which we call the precision grip. This grip is used, for example, in holding a pen or a paintbrush. With this grip, you have much greater control over what you are holding. The object is usually held by the soft parts of the **fingertips** (below the **fingernails**) of the first three fingers — the thumb, the **index finger** and the **middle finger**. With this grip, the **little finger** (or **pinky**) and the **ring finger** do nothing.

The development of the precision grip was important. It made it possible for humans to become tool makers, and so humans became the first and only animals to create and use technology.

## Exercise 1

Choose the best answer according to the passage.

1  Millions of years ago, prehistoric people could hold things
   a)  in one way    b)  in two ways    c)  in more than two ways

2  How has the human hand changed?
   a)  the wrist moves differently    b)  there are now five fingers    c)  it can grip differently

3  When you use the power grip, you hold something with
   a)  all five fingers    b)  four fingers    c)  three fingers

4  When you use the precision grip, you hold something with
   a)  all five fingers    b)  four fingers    c)  three fingers

5  Why is the precision grip important in human history?
   a)  People could make tools.    b)  People could write and paint.    c)  People could hold things.

## Exercise 2

*Name the parts of the hand in these pictures.*

| thumb | middle finger | palm | ring finger | wrist | fingernail | index finger | fingertip | pinky |

1 _____

2 _____

3 _____

4 _____

5 _____

6 _____

7 _____

8 _____

9 _____

## Exercise 3

*Answer these questions with the parts of the hand and arm given below.*

| a) wrist | b) elbows | c) thumb | d) nails |

1 A baby may put it in its mouth and suck it. _____

2 Some people bite them, especially if they are nervous. _____

3 You wear your watch on it. _____

4 Some people think you should not put them on the table while eating. _____

## Just for fun

*See if you can do these things with your hands. Then compare your actions with other people's.*

1 Touch your wrist with your thumb.
2 Hold all the fingers of your hand straight up. Bend the pinky down without moving the other fingers.
3 Bend the top part of your index finger, keeping the rest of the finger straight.
4 Make a loud noise by pressing your middle finger against your thumb.

## Think about

1 Do people wear special rings on special fingers in your country?
2 In the U.S., if you put your thumb up in the air it means that everything is all right. Do you use hand gestures in your country? What do they mean?

3 What do you think these idioms mean?
   a) To hold someone in the palm of your hand.
   b) To have everything at your fingertips.
   c) To keep your fingers crossed.
   d) To be all thumbs.

# 1.8 Ways of touching and holding

**Words in context**   *Read the following passage and do the exercises.*

Detective Jones sat at her desk and studied the three photographs. In the first picture, a man was playing tennis. The second picture showed the same man eating in a restaurant. In the third picture, the man was lying on the floor, **holding** a gun in his hand. He was dead and it looked as if he had shot himself. But was it really suicide? There was something wrong with this picture and Detective Jones didn't know what it was.

You could always tell when Detective Jones was thinking hard because her hands never stopped moving. She was thinking now, as she studied the three photos carefully.

She **scratched** the top of her head with her long fingernails. She **stroked** her chin with her thumb and index finger as though she were stroking a long beard. She put both her hands on the back of her neck and **massaged** it, **rubbing** hard into the muscle, trying to make herself relax. "Now what is wrong with these photographs?" she kept asking herself. "What is it?"

She **tapped** the desk with her fingers as she tought. Then, suddenly, she could see what was wrong. She **slapped** the side of her leg with her open hand, raised her right hand in a fist and **punched** the air. "Of course," she said. "Of course, I've got it."

She **grabbed** the telephone and called Detective Sanchez. "He's going to be very surprised," she said to herself, as she **gripped** the telephone with excitement, waiting for him to answer.

"Detective Sanchez," she said, "Hello. It's me, Detective Jones. Listen. The man was murdered. Look at the hands in the three photographs. Can you see what's wrong?"

## Exercise 1

*Put these pictures of Detective Jones in the right order according to the passage.*

1 ____   2 ____   3 ____   4 ____   5 ____   6 ____   7 ____   8 ____

How did Detective Jones know that the man had been murdered?

## Exercise 2

Use these words to fill in the blanks.

| a) punch | b) massage | c) slap | d) rub | e) grip | f) stroke | g) grab | h) tap |

1 Somebody trying to get your attention might _____ you on the shoulder.

2 A boxer in a fight will try to _____ his opponent.

3 Someone who says something very rude might get a _____ on the face.

4 Somebody trying to make a cat feel good might _____ its back.

5 A tired football player may want someone to _____ his legs.

6 A tennis player has to _____ the tennis racket.

7 A hungry cat will _____ its back against your legs.

8 A greedy child will _____ the last piece of cake.

## Dictionary work

These words all describe actions performed with the hands. Can you match the actions to the pictures?
Do as many as you can and then check your answers in a dictionary.

| a) push | b) shake | c) catch | d) pull | e) scratch | f) ring | g) punch | h) clap |
| i) pat | j) point | k) strangle | l) tickle | m) squeeze | n) wave | o) grip |

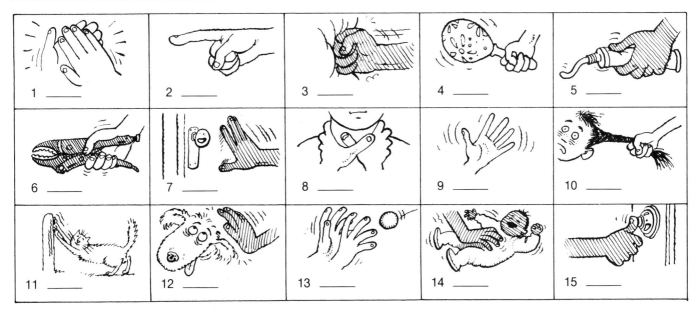

## Think about

1 Are there different sports in which you fight with your hands in your country? Can you describe them?

2 How can you get someone's attention? Describe the different ways.

3 Can you guess the meaning of these idioms?
   a) Try not to rub him the wrong way.
   b) This book is really gripping.
   c) Her decision was a real slap in the face.

# 1.9 Legs and feet

## Words in context

*Read the following passage and do the exercises.*

At the hospital, Bill took off his sock and pulled his pants leg up over his **knee** onto his **thigh**. The doctor looked down at the injured **foot** which was already getting bigger and changing color.

"Hm. Nasty accident," he said. "What happened?"

"A skier smashed into my foot," explained Bill.

"Oh, dear. Very nasty. Well, let's see what's wrong, shall we?"

The doctor gently picked up Bill's foot, and taking the **heel** in the palm of his left hand, he slowly moved the **toes**, testing each one. The **big toe** looked the worst. The **toenail** was badly broken and it was bleeding a little. Then, putting his right hand under Bill's **calf** and still holding the heel in his left hand, he moved the foot gently from side to side.

"Does your **ankle** hurt when I do that?" the doctor asked.

"Not too much," Bill answered.

The doctor looked up. "Good. Well, Mr. Harvey, you are very lucky. Nothing is broken and you should be fine again in a few days' time."

"Will I be able to ski then?" asked Bill.

"Oh, yes. Of course you will," answered the doctor.

"That's good," said Bill, "because I don't know how to ski now!"

## Exercise 1

*Decide whether the following statements are true (T) or false (F) according to the passage.*

1 _____ Bill took off his sock so that the doctor could examine his foot.

2 _____ Bill also took off his pants.

3 _____ The doctor examined all five of Bill's toes.

4 _____ The big toe was injured the most.

5 _____ All five toenails were broken.

6 _____ The doctor supported Bill's heel with his left hand while he examined his foot.

7 _____ The doctor moved Bill's foot from side to side to see if his calf was all right.

8 _____ In a few days, Bill will know how to ski.

## Exercise 2

*Name the parts of the leg and foot in the picture.*

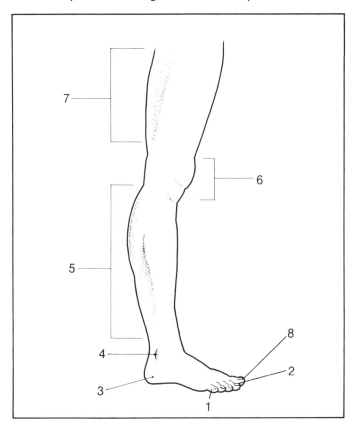

| knee | calf | ankle | heel |
|------|------|-------|------|
| toenail | toe | thigh | big toe |

1 _____

2 _____

3 _____

4 _____

5 _____

6 _____

7 _____

8 _____

## Just for fun

*These twelve words are hidden in this word square. The words are written forwards, backwards, diagonally, up or down. How quickly can you find them?*

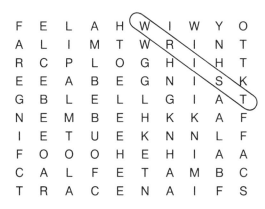

```
F  E  L  A  H  W  I  W  Y  O
A  L  I  M  T  W  R  I  N  T
R  C  P  L  O  G  H  I  H  T
E  E  A  B  E  G  N  I  S  K
G  B  L  E  L  L  G  I  A  T
N  E  M  B  E  H  K  K  A  F
I  E  T  U  E  K  N  N  L  F
F  O  O  O  H  E  H  I  A  A
C  A  L  F  E  T  A  M  B  C
T  R  A  C  E  N  A  I  F  S
```

| calf | nail | toe | wrist |
|------|------|-----|-------|
| ankle | palm | knee | thumb |
| thigh | finger | heel | elbow |

## Think about

1  In which sports are leg and foot injuries particularly common? Why?
   Have you ever had a sports injury? What happened?

2  Which exercises are good for strengthening the legs?

3  What do you think these idioms mean?
   a)  To put your foot in your mouth.   b)  To get cold feet.
   c)  To keep your feet on the ground.

# 1.10 Ways of moving

**Words in context**   *Read the following passages and do the exercises.*

Roberto couldn't get to sleep. He didn't know why. At two o'clock in the morning he decided to go downstairs and get some food. Everyone in the house was asleep so he **tiptoed** down the stairs, making as little noise as possible. (Now answer question 1, Exercise 1.)

From the hotel window, you could see the green hills covered with tall trees, and in the distance was a little lake.
    "Let's put on some boots, take some sandwiches and spend the day **hiking** in the mountains," their father said. (Now answer question 4.)

It was a dark day and it looked as if it might rain. From the hotel window, you could see the beach. No one was there.
    "Let's **wander** around the town and get to know this place a little better," their father suggested. (Now answer question 6.)

Jim and Sandy had met on vacation and were very much in love. This was their last day together. Now, as the sun went down over the sea, they **strolled** hand in hand along the beach, looking into each other's eyes, saying nothing. (Now answer question 2.)

The boxer took a hard punch on the chin. He stood still for a second and then his legs became weak. Almost falling, he started to **stagger** like a drunken man. One more punch and he was down . . . seven, eight, nine, ten. It was a knock-out. (Now answer question 7.)

"Oh no," shouted Mike, "my contact lens fell out." Soon everyone was on their hands and knees, **crawling** around looking for it.
    "You can all stand up now," someone said. "I found it." (Now answer question 3.)

The boys were seventeen years old and they were in the Army. Every day they had to practice **marching** as the sergeant called out, "Left, right. Left, right. Left." (Now answer question 5.)

In the village, most people were happily getting ready to go skiing. There were only a few people who looked unhappy. They could not go skiing. They had each injured a leg, a knee or an ankle, and were now **limping** around the village with nothing to do. (Now answer question 8.)

## Exercise 1

*Decide whether the following statements are true (T) or false (F) according to the passages.*

1 _____ Roberto walked on the tips of his toes to make no noise.

2 _____ Jim and Sandy walked very fast along the beach.

3 _____ The contact lens fell on the floor.

4 _____ Their father suggested a long walk in the countryside.

5 _____ Every time the sergeant said "Left," the boys had to put down their left foot.

6 _____ Their father suggested going to a special place in the town.

7 _____ The boxer was staggering because he had been drinking before the fight.

8 _____ The people who looked unhappy did not like skiing.

## Exercise 2

*Match each of these verbs with its meaning. Put an X in the right box, as in the example.*

|  | stroll | wander | march | limp | hike | tiptoe | stagger | crawl |
|---|---|---|---|---|---|---|---|---|
| with each step equal |  |  | X |  |  |  |  |  |
| quietly, on your toes |  |  |  |  |  |  |  |  |
| stepping harder on one foot than the other |  |  |  |  |  |  |  |  |
| in a slow, relaxed way |  |  |  |  |  |  |  |  |
| in an unsteady way |  |  |  |  |  |  |  |  |
| in the countryside |  |  |  |  |  |  |  |  |
| on your hands and knees |  |  |  |  |  |  |  |  |
| in no particular direction |  |  |  |  |  |  |  |  |

## Exercise 3

*How do these people walk? (Choose from the words in **Exercise 2**.)*

1 A soldier _____

2 A thief _____

3 Someone who is drunk _____

4 Someone who is lost _____

5 A six-month-old baby _____

6 An old couple in a park _____

## Dictionary work

*Some of these words describe leg movements and some describe actions that are performed with the hands and arms. Write (L) next to the leg movements and (H) next to hand actions. Do as many as you can and then check your answers in a dictionary.*

1 _____ kick

2 _____ hug

3 _____ clap

4 _____ draw

5 _____ dash

6 _____ box

7 _____ skate

8 _____ point

9 _____ jump

10 _____ throw

11 _____ trip over

12 _____ stamp

13 _____ type

14 _____ dance

15 _____ cycle

## Think about

1 Do you like hiking? Where have you gone hiking?
2 How old are most babies when they start crawling? When do they usually start walking?
3 Walking is good exercise. How much walking do you do every day?

# Vocabulary review

## 1.6 Body size and body parts

average
back
big
blood
bone
brain
broad
buttocks
chest
fat
feet
heart
height
hip
intestines
liver
lungs
muscle
narrow
neck
overweight
short
shoulder
skin
skinny
slim
small
strong
tall
thin
waist
weak
well-built

## 1.7 Arms and hands

arm
elbow
finger
fingernail
fingertip
hand
index finger
little finger
middle finger
palm
pinky
ring finger
thumb
wrist

## 1.8 Ways of touching and holding

catch
clap
grab
grip
hold
massage
pat
point
pull
punch
push
ring
rub
scratch
shake
slap
squeeze
strangle
stroke
tap
tickle
wave

## 1.9 Legs and feet

ankle
big toe
calf
foot
heel
knee
leg
thigh
toe
toenail

## 1.10 Ways of moving

box
clap
crawl
cycle
dance
dash
draw
hike
hug
jump
kick
limp
march
point
skate
stagger
stamp
stroll
throw
tiptoe
trip over
type
wander

# Test yourself 2

■■■■■■■■■■■■■■■■■■■■■■■■■■■■■■■■■■■■■■■■■■■■■■■■■■■■■■■■■■■■■■

Use the words from the **Vocabulary review** to help you fill the blanks in these sentences.
In some cases you have been given the last letter of the word. More than one answer may be
possible, but there is usually one best answer.

1 It takes a long time for a ballet dancer to learn to dance on the tips of her _____.

2 "Oh, there's some _____d on the kitchen table."

3 "Yes, I cut my _____r with a sharp knife while I was cutting vegetables."

4 My doctor told me I was _____, so I'm only going to eat fruit for the next month.

5 It is not unusual to injure your _____w if you play too much tennis.

6 Before I buy Christmas presents, I like to _____r around the stores and get some ideas first.

7 The man in front of me in the theater kept talking, so I _____ him on the

8 _____r and asked him to be quiet.

9 When Mr. Jones looked at his _____, he saw that his watch was not there.
   He realized he must have left it on the beach.

10 The little boy _____d his mother's hand the whole time they were on the plane,

11 while she _____ his head and told him not to worry.

12 I can't stop _____ myself. I was almost eaten to death by mosquitoes last night in
   my bedroom.

13 I didn't see the cat as I entered the house. I _____ _____ it and

14 fell down and cut my _____e.

15 She's so _____m. She has a beautiful,

16 _____ waist and a very flat stomach. She must do a lot of exercise.

17 As the train left the station, Helena leaned out of the window and _____.
   "Goodbye," she said. "Goodbye."

18 Tommy, your grandfather dropped his glasses under the table. Can you _____
   under there and get them for him?

19 "How did you break the _____ on your little finger?"

20 "I broke it trying to _____h a baseball."

21 I can't go _____ with you in the mountains tomorrow, because yesterday

22 I hurt my _____e while I was climbing.

23 The football player had very big _____h muscles.

24 Take a deep breath and fill your _____ with the clean mountain air.

25 Come on everybody, I want you to _____p your hands in time to the music.

# 2 The inner self

## 2.1 Happiness and sadness

**Words in context**

*Read the following passage and do the exercises.*

Mr. Simms never smiled. He lived in a small town where everyone was always **in a good mood** — everyone except him. He always seemed to be **miserable** and liked to make other people miserable too.

One day, while Mr. Simms was on his way to the bank, he met Mrs. Toogood. It was a beautiful sunny day and Mrs. Toogood felt great. "Well, good morning Mr. Simms. What's the matter? You look so **depressed**. Did you get some bad news?" she asked him.

"No, I'm fine, thank you, Mrs. Toogood," he said.

"Well, you shouldn't look so miserable, Mr. Simms, on such a lovely sunny day."

"It's sunny now," said Mr. Simms, "but it will probably rain later."

"Nonsense," said Mrs. Toogood and she walked on. (Now answer questions 1, 2 and 3 in Exercise 1.)

Next, Mr. Simms walked past the flower shop where Miss Lightheart was putting out some lovely fresh flowers. "Good morning, Mr. Simms. Is everything all right? You look so **sad**. No deaths in the family, I hope."

"No. Everything's fine thank you, Miss Lightheart."

"Well then, you shouldn't be looking so **unhappy** on such a beautiful day, Mr. Simms."

"It could rain later, you know," said Mr. Simms.

"It could rain."

"I don't think so Mr. Simms. Goodbye, sir."(Now answer questions 4 and 5.)

Mr. Simms went to the bank where the bank manager, Mr. Freebody, gave him a large friendly smile. "Did you lose some money, Mr. Simms? You look so **upset**."

"There's nothing wrong with me," said Mr. Simms, "but tell me, why are you in such a good mood? You look very **cheerful** and **pleased** with life."

"Look outside," said Mr. Freebody. "It's such a nice day today."

"Hm. I wouldn't be surprised if it rained later," said Mr. Simms. "I wouldn't be surprised at all."

"Not today, Mr. Simms. Not today. And how much money would you like?" (Now answer question 6.)

Mr. Simms took his money and went home. As usual, he didn't look at all **happy**. He took his newspaper, sat down, and started to read. He read for about an hour, when suddenly he noticed that the room was a little dark. There was a noise at the window and Mr. Simms looked out. He couldn't believe it. He was absolutely **delighted** and a big smile appeared on his face. (Now answer question 7.)

## Exercise 1

*Give short answers to these questions*

1 Where was Mr. Simms going? _____

2 Why was Mrs. Toogood in such a good mood? _____

3 Why did Mrs. Toogood ask Mr. Simms if he had gotten any bad news? _____

4 Where did Miss Lightheart work? _____

5 What sort of weather did Mr. Simms expect later in the day? _____

6 Why did Mr. Freebody think Mr. Simms was upset? _____

7 Why did Mr. Simms finally smile? _____

## Exercise 2

Divide these sentences into two groups. Put all the "happy" sentences in the first column and all the "unhappy" sentences in the second column.

a) I feel miserable.

b) I feel cheerful.

c) I'm really depressed.

d) I'm in a good mood.

e) I'm really pleased.

f) I'm absolutely delighted.

g) I'm upset.

h) I feel sad.

_____ _____

_____ _____

_____ _____

_____ _____

## Exercise 3

Complete the crossword puzzle. Each answer describes how you might feel in these situations.

**Across**

2 Your boy/girlfriend leaves you. (7)
4 You have a really nice surprise. (9)
6 Someone says they don't like you. (5)
8 You are feeling very sick. (9)
9 You got some great news. (2, 1, 4, 4)

**Down**

1 Everything is going well. (8)
3 Everything is going wrong. (9)
5 Your boy/girlfriend says he/she loves you. (5)
7 Your dog dies. (3)

## Dictionary work

Here is a list of things you might do if you were feeling cheerful or depressed.
Write (C) next to the cheerful actions and (D) next to depressed actions.
Do as many as you can and then check your answers in a dictionary.

1 _____ cry

2 _____ smile

3 _____ sulk

4 _____ frown

5 _____ sing

6 _____ burst into tears

7 _____ sigh

8 _____ pout

9 _____ dance

10 _____ tell a joke

11 _____ grin

12 _____ whistle

13 _____ laugh

14 _____ complain

15 _____ groan

## Think about

1 What puts you in a good mood?
2 What makes you cry?
3 What makes people laugh? Can you tell a joke in English?
4 Do you sometimes feel depressed? What do you do to make yourself feel better?

# 2.2 Stress and anger

## Words in context   *Read the following passage and do the exercises.*

Every day you read in newspapers, books and magazines that it is important to avoid stress. Stress can kill, they say. Stay **calm**. Be **relaxed**. Slow down. Don't worry so much and don't work so hard. Unfortunately, this is difficult. There are always money problems and family problems. Our cities are full of traffic and noise. Stressful situations seem to be everywhere.

When people are **under stress** they react in different ways. Some people find it difficult to stay calm and often become **tense**. Little things, like a baby crying, can make them **irritated**. They get very **annoyed** if they have to wait just a few minutes too long in a store or a restaurant. These people are usually very **moody**. One minute they are fine and the next they can be really **angry** — absolutely **furious**. Other people seem to stay calm almost all the time, and rarely get angry. For example, if they are caught in bad traffic, they don't get **frustrated**. They sit calmly in their cars, telling themselves that there is nothing they can do about the situation. These people are not moody at all. They don't change from moment to moment, but always seem to be in control of their emotions.

Some doctors give names to these two personality types: Type A people and Type B people. Type As work very hard, worry a lot, and are often **bad-tempered**. Type Bs are the opposite. They don't worry. Work is not so important to them and they don't get angry easily. They like to relax a lot and have fun. These doctors say it is better for your health and your heart if you are a Type B person. So what are you? Type A or Type B?

## Exercise 1

*Decide whether these characteristics belong to a Type A or a Type B person according to the information in the passage. Then write the letters in the blanks below.*

a)  is moody
b)  seldom relaxes
c)  stays calm
d)  is not annoyed by a baby crying
e)  gets frustrated in traffic
f)  enjoys life and work
g)  is usually in a good mood

h)  overworks
i)  lives longer
j)  doesn't get tense
k)  worries a lot
l)  doesn't like waiting
m) is relaxed
n)  is often bad-tempered

**Type A**

\_\_\_\_  \_\_\_\_  \_\_\_\_  \_\_\_\_  \_\_\_\_  \_\_\_\_  \_\_\_\_

**Type B**

\_\_\_\_  \_\_\_\_  \_\_\_\_  \_\_\_\_  \_\_\_\_  \_\_\_\_  \_\_\_\_

## Exercise 2

Put these words in order from least angry (1) to most angry (5).

| a) annoyed | b) calm | c) furious | d) irritated | e) angry |
|---|---|---|---|---|

 1 ____  2 ____  3 ____  4 ____  5 ____

## Exercise 3

Use one of these words or phrases to describe each person.

| a) frustrated | b) bad-tempered | c) moody | d) tense | e) calm | f) under stress |
|---|---|---|---|---|---|

1 Someone who can be happy one moment and unhappy the next. _____

2 Someone who finds it difficult to relax. _____

3 Someone who does not get excited when there are problems. _____

4 Someone who cannot do what he or she wants to do. _____

5 Someone who often gets angry. _____

6 Someone who is always busy and has a lot of problems. _____

## Just for fun

How would you feel in these situations? Compare your answers with other people's.

1 You just missed a bus or a train.
2 You cannot find something, but you know it's somewhere in your house.
3 You cannot sleep because your neighbor is playing very loud music.
4 Your friend arrives forty minutes late for dinner.
5 You have to work or study on a beautiful sunny day.
6 You have to wait in a traffic jam.
7 You are sitting near someone who is smoking while you are eating.
8 You have nothing at all to do.

*irritated*   *furious*   *frustrated*   *tense*   *angry*   *annoyed*   *calm*

## Think about

1 What makes you angry?

2 Do you think you have a Type A personality or a Type B personality? Why?

3 Do you agree with the doctors who say that it is bad to have a Type A personality? Why? Why not?

4 What can you do to become a more relaxed person?

# 2.3 Fear

■■■■■■■■■■■■■■■■■■■■■■■■■■■■■■■■■■■■■■■■■■■■■■■■■■■■■■■■

### Words in context

*Read the following passages and do the exercises.*

"Are you a man or a mouse?" When people ask this question they want to know if you think you are a **brave** person or a **coward**. But you will never really know the answer to that question until you are tested in real life. Some people think they are brave, but when they come face to face with real danger, they act like cowards. Other people think of themselves as **cowardly**, but when they meet danger, act like **heroes**. (Now answer questions 1, 2 and 3 in Exercise 1.)

Lenny Skutnik had always thought of himself as a **nervous** person. He got **worried** before exams. He worried about his job and his health. All he wanted in life was to be **safe** and healthy. Then, on January 15, 1982, a plane crashed into the Potomac River in Washington. Lenny went to the river to see what was happening. The he saw a woman in the ice-cold water. Suddenly Lenny did not feel **afraid**. He kept very **calm** and did a very **courageous** thing. He jumped into the Potomac, swam to the woman, and kept her head above the water. Seventy-eight people died that day. Thanks to Lenny Skutnik, it was not seventy-nine. (Now answer questions 4, 5 and 6.)

When you are in a very **dangerous** situation and feel afraid, the body automatically produces a chemical in the blood. This chemical is called adrenalin. With adrenalin in the blood system, you actually feel stronger and are ready to fight or run away. However, when you are absolutely **terrified**, the body can produce too much adrenalin. When this happens, the muscles become very hard and you find out that you cannot move at all. You are then paralyzed with fear. That is why, when we are very **frightened**, we sometimes say that we are **"petrified."** This word comes from the Greek word "petros," which means "stone." We are so frightened we become like stone. (Now answer questions 7, 8 and 9.)

## Exercise 1

*Decide whether these statements are true (T) or false (F) according to the passage.*

1 _____ If people think you are a "mouse," they think you are a coward.

2 _____ Some people like to think of themselves as brave people.

3 _____ If you think of yourself as cowardly, you will never act like a hero.

4 _____ Lenny Skutnik was often nervous and worried.

5 _____ Lenny did not feel afraid when he swam to the woman in the water.

6 _____ Lenny was a passenger on that plane.

7 _____ People who feel afraid take a drug called adrenalin.

8 _____ A certain amount of adrenalin makes us feel strong.

9 _____ The Greek word "petros" means "terrified."

## Exercise 2

Find four pairs of words which are similar in meaning and use them to fill in the chart.

| | |
|---|---|
| and | |
| and | |
| and | |
| and | |

| | |
|---|---|
| nervous | brave |
| afraid | terrified |
| petrified | courageous |
| worried | frightened |

Find four pairs of words which are almost opposite in meaning and use them to fill in the chart.

| | |
|---|---|
| and | |
| and | |
| and | |
| and | |

| | |
|---|---|
| cowardly | dangerous |
| safe | calm |
| coward | nervous |
| hero | brave |

## Just for fun

Think about these situations. How afraid would you be in each case?
Add up your scores and find out how brave you are.

|  | calm | | nervous | | afraid | | terrified | |
|---|---|---|---|---|---|---|---|---|
| Walking past an angry dog | 0 | 1 | 2 | 3 | 4 | 5 | 6 | 7 |
| Being alone at night in a house | 0 | 1 | 2 | 3 | 4 | 5 | 6 | 7 |
| Seeing a mouse in the kitchen | 0 | 1 | 2 | 3 | 4 | 5 | 6 | 7 |
| Seeing a spider in the bathroom | 0 | 1 | 2 | 3 | 4 | 5 | 6 | 7 |
| Flying in an airplane | 0 | 1 | 2 | 3 | 4 | 5 | 6 | 7 |
| Watching a horror movie | 0 | 1 | 2 | 3 | 4 | 5 | 6 | 7 |
| Holding a snake in your hand | 0 | 1 | 2 | 3 | 4 | 5 | 6 | 7 |
| Going 90 mph on a motorcycle | 0 | 1 | 2 | 3 | 4 | 5 | 6 | 7 |
| Talking to a group of a hundred people | 0 | 1 | 2 | 3 | 4 | 5 | 6 | 7 |

What is your total? If you score 0–20, you are a very brave person; if you score 20–40, you are quite normal; if you score 40–60, don't be such a coward!

## Think about

1 What frightens you most? Do you know people who have strange fears?

2 What are the differences between adult fears and children's fears?

3 Can fear be enjoyable? What do people do to make themselves afraid?

4 What methods are there for helping people who have strong fears?

# 2.4 Love and loving

Sally Jones is fifteen years old and has never been in love. She likes boys. She goes out with them and sometimes she even kisses them. There are several boys she is interested in, and there are several boys who like her. But she has never felt true love for anyone. And, oh, how she wants to adore someone and be adored, the way it is in the movies. She is very worried. Maybe, she thinks, there is something wrong with her. Maybe she will never fall in love. Maybe, and this is the worst possibility of all, there is no such thing as true love.

Her friend, Barbara, is very different. She is always falling in and out of love and goes out with a different boy each week. Last week she was madly, passionately, in love with Mickey. This week she has decided to stop seeing Mickey and is dating Jim, who she is crazy about. Next week she probably won't care about Jim any more, but will be going out with Dave. She likes Dave and is very attracted to him.

## Exercise 1

*Choose the best answer according to the passage.*

1 Sally Jones is worried because
  a) she doesn't like boys
  b) boys don't like her
  c) she can't fall in love

2 Sally thinks
  a) her life is like a romantic movie
  b) she may be different from other girls
  c) true love comes only once in your life

3 This week Barbara is in love with
  a) Mickey
  b) Jim
  c) Dave

4 How does Barbara feel about Dave?
  a) She is in love with him.
  b) She would like to go out with him.
  c) She is not attracted to him.

## Exercise 2

Match each phrase in the first column with a phrase in the second column which has almost the same meaning.

1 _____ to date

2 _____ to care about

3 _____ to be crazy about

4 _____ to fall out of love with

a) to adore

b) to go out with

c) to be interested in

d) to stop loving

## Exercise 3

What are some of the things that couples do to show their love? Match each verb in the first column with the most likely phrase in the second column.

1 _____ hold

2 _____ look

3 _____ kiss

4 _____ walk

5 _____ put

a) into each other's eyes

b) their arms around each other

c) hands

d) passionately

e) arm in arm

## Dictionary work

Look at these items and put them in the right columns. Do as many as you can and then check your answers in a dictionary.

| | | | |
|---|---|---|---|
| roses | candlelight | soft music | cocktails |
| beaches | jewelery | gardens | parks |
| moonlight | forests | firelight | perfume |
| champagne | diamonds | chocolates | wine |

| **romantic places** | **romantic gifts** | **romantic food and drink** | **romantic light and music** |
|---|---|---|---|
| _____ | _____ | _____ | _____ |
| _____ | _____ | _____ | _____ |
| _____ | _____ | _____ | _____ |
| _____ | _____ | _____ | _____ |

Can you add to these lists?

## Think about

1  What advice would you give Sally Jones?
2  Do you believe in true love? Are there different types of love?
3  What do you think these English expressions mean?
   a) Love is blind.   b) Love me, love my dog.   c) All is fair in love and war.

# 2.5 Marriage

**Words in context**  *Read the following passage and do the exercises.*

Dolores Valentine knows all about love. She is sixty-five years old and has **been married** six times. The first time she was a **bride**, her **wedding** day was on her seventeenth birthday. The last time she got married, she was sixty-two. Her **groom** that day was seventy-five and he died two weeks later.

Dolores Valentine has been married six times, but the remarkable thing is that she has never **been divorced**. All six of her **husbands** died while they were married to her. Six times she has been a loving **wife** and six times she has been left a **widow**.

Now she is **engaged** again and is going to be married in six weeks' time. But this time she is going to marry a man much younger than herself. Her **fiancé** is a thirty-nine-year old farmer—strong and healthy. This time Dolores feels pretty sure that she is going to be the one to die first and leave her husband a **widower**. But Dolores isn't worried. Until then, she is going to have a good time and enjoy life, because Dolores knows that you are only as old as you feel.

## Exercise 1

*Fill the blanks in these sentences with the correct information according to the passage.*

1  Dolores was a _____ on the day she turned seventeen.

2  Dolores' last husband died at the age of _____ .

3  Dolores has been married, but never _____ .

4  Dolores has been a widow _____ times.

5  Dolores is now _____ to a farmer.

6  Dolores' _____ is thirty-nine years old.

7  Dolores' next _____ day will be in six weeks.

8  Dolores will become the _____ of a younger man.

9  The farmer will be Dolores' seventh _____ .

10  Dolores expects that the farmer will one day be a _____ .

## Exercise 2

*Put these words in the right boxes in the chart.*

| widower | boyfriend | bride | husband | fiancé |
|---------|-----------|-------|---------|--------|
| fiancée | girlfriend | wife | **groom** | widow |

|  | **male** | **female** |
|---|---|---|
| The person you are going out with |  |  |
| The person you are engaged to |  |  |
| The person on the day of his/her wedding |  |  |
| The person you are married to |  |  |
| The person left after the death of the husband/wife |  |  |

## Exercise 3

*Can you put these events into the right order?*

1  First, Jim and Olga _____       a)  got married

2  Then, they _____              b)  fell in love

3  So, they _____                c)  met

4  Not long after that, they _____   d)  got divorced

5  A few years later, they _____    e)  got engaged

6  So, finally they _____          f)  fell out of love

## Just for fun

*What makes a successful marriage? Put this list in order from most important (1) to least important (5) and compare your answers with other people's.*

_____  being close in age                    _____  having the same nationality

_____  having the same hobbies and leisure interests   _____  having the same religion

_____  having the same educational background   *What else is important for a successful marriage?*

## Think about

1  What do you think is the best age to get married?
   At what age do people usually get married in your country?

2  Do you think it is better to marry someone older or younger than yourself? Why?

3  In your country, who usually keeps the children if the parents get a divorce?

# Vocabulary review

## 2 The inner self (Units 2.1–2.5)

### 2.1 Happiness and sadness

burst into tears
cheerful
complain
cry
dance
delighted
depressed
frown
grin
groan
happy
in a good mood
joke
laugh
miserable
pleased
pout
sad
sigh
sing
smile
sulk
unhappy
upset
whistle

### 2.2 Stress and anger

angry
annoyed
bad-tempered
calm
frustrated
furious
irritated
moody
relaxed
tense
under stress

### 2.3 Fear

afraid
brave
calm
courageous
coward
cowardly
dangerous
frightened
hero
nervous
petrified
safe
terrified
worried

### 2.4 Love and loving

adore
beach
be attracted to
be crazy about
be (madly) in love with
be interested in
candlelight
care about
champagne
chocolate
cocktail
date
diamond
fall in/out of love with
firelight
forest
garden
go out with
jewelry
kiss
moonlight
music
park
perfume
rose
soft
wine

### 2.5 Marriage

be/get divorced
be/get engaged
be/get married
bride
fiancé(e)
groom
husband
wedding
widow
widower
wife

# Test yourself 3

■■■■■■■■■■■■■■■■■■■■■■■■■■■■■■■■■■■■■■■■■■■■■■■■■■■

Use the words from the **Vocabulary review** to help you fill the blanks in these sentences.
In some cases you have been given the last letter of the word. More than one answer may be
possible, but there is usually one best answer.

1 "How old were you when you first _____ in love?"

2 "Well, I don't know if it was love, but when I was seventeen I was absolutely _____
   about a French man who was ten years older than me."

3 The day after her husband died, the sixty-year-old _____ told her family that she

4 _____ _____ her husband but never really loved him.

5 I have had a lot of problems recently and have felt under a lot of _____.

6 On the day of the _____g there was a full moon. The young

7 _____ and her groom were married in the evening, outside in the

8 _____t in the garden. It was so romantic.

9 I had to wait thirty minutes in the store. When I was finally helped I was so _____d.
   I told the clerk that I no longer wanted anything.

10 When I get _____d, I don't talk, I don't smile, I don't laugh. I just like to sleep a lot.

11 At the end of the summer, when they had to say goodbye, they both burst into _____.

12 "We shouldn't be so _____y," he said. "We'll see each other again, I'm sure."

13 I think I'm a _____d. If I saw people fighting in the street, I wouldn't try to stop
   them because I might get hurt.

14 They were _____ for four months. Then one day he told his fiancée that he didn't want to
   get married.

15 She was so _____d of her husband that it took her six years to get up the courage

16 to tell him that she wanted to get _____d because she did not love him anymore.

17 "You look very _____d. What's the problem?"

18 "I'm about to give a speech to a hundred people and I'm so _____s."

19 I am in a very good _____ today. You see, there is a girl that I am

20 _____ to, and I heard that she likes me too.

21 People who are very _____y are very difficult to live with. They can be happy and

22 smiling one minute, and miserable and _____ _____ the next.

23 I am not a very _____ person. I get nervous flying in airplanes, even though people

24 keep telling me that it's _____r to travel in a plane than in a car.

25 People get very _____ when they find that they can't speak English perfectly
   after studying it for years.

# 2.6 Intelligence

**Words in context** *Read the following passage and do the exercises.*

What makes one person more **intelligent** than another? What makes one person a **genius**, like the **brilliant** Albert Einstein, and another person a **fool**? Are people born intelligent or **stupid**, or is intelligence the result of where and how you live? These are very old questions and the answers to them are still not clear.

We know, however, that just being born with a good mind is not enough. In some ways, the mind is like a leg or an arm muscle. It needs exercise. Mental exercise is particularly important for young children. Many child psychologists think that parents should play with their children more often and give them problems to think about. The children are then more likely to grow up **bright** and intelligent. If, on the other hand, children are left alone a great deal with nothing to do, they are more likely to become **slow** and **unintelligent**.

Parents should also be careful what they say to young children. According to some psychologists, if parents are always telling a child that he or she is a fool or an **idiot**, then the child is more likely to keep doing **silly** and **foolish** things. So it is probably better for parents to say very positive

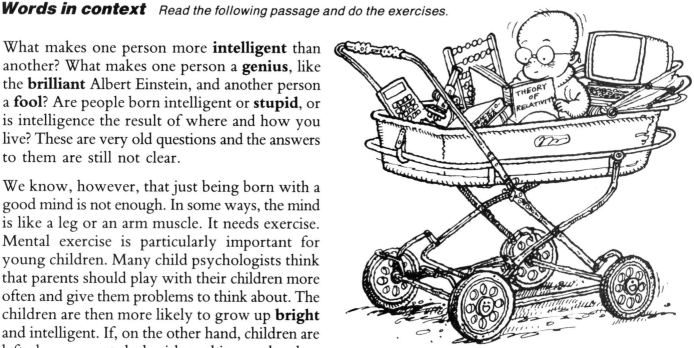

things to their children, such as "That was a very **clever** thing you did" or "You are such a **smart** child."

What do you think? Are people born intelligent or do they become intelligent with the help of good parents and teachers?

## Exercise 1

*Change the words in dark print to make the sentences true, according to the passage.*

1 Einstein was very **stupid**. _____

2 The more you **rest** your mind, the more intelligent you should become. _____

3 Parents should **never** play with their children. _____

4 Children who are always left alone are more likely to be **bright**. _____

5 It is bad for parents to tell children that they are **smart**. _____

6 Parents should say very **negative** things to their children. _____

## Exercise 2

Put each word in one of the four columns, depending on whether it is an adjective or a noun meaning "intelligent" or "unintelligent."

| idiot | clever | bright | foolish | fool | genius | slow | brilliant | silly |

| intelligent (adj) | unintelligent (adj) | intelligent person (n) | unintelligent person (n) |
|---|---|---|---|
| 1 | 4 | 7 | 8 |
| 2 | 5 | | 9 |
| 3 | 6 | | |

## Exercise 3

Mr. and Mrs. Einstein have very bright children because they always talk to them in a very positive way. Mr. and Mrs. Potatohead have children that are not so bright, perhaps because they criticize their children a lot. Which parents are talking to the children in these sentences?

a) "You little genius."
b) "That wasn't a very smart thing to do."
c) "I can't believe you could be so unintelligent."
d) "That was brilliant."
e) "What a bright child you are."

f) "What a smart little boy."
g) "You little idiot."
h) "You're such an intelligent little girl."
i) "You stupid fool."
j) "How could you do such a foolish thing?"

1   The Einsteins

2   The Potatoheads

____   ____   ____   ____   ____          ____   ____   ____   ____   ____

## Just for fun

Can you solve these intelligence problems?

1 Try to join the nine dots by drawing only four straight lines and never taking your pencil off the paper.

2 Move the three blocks from the first tower to the last tower so that the blocks are in the same order. You can only move one block at a time, and you can never place a larger block on top of a smaller one.

3 If four days before tomorrow is Thursday, what is three days after yesterday? _____

## Think about

1 Do you know any intelligence problems?
2 Do intelligent people always do well at school? Why? Why not?
3 What is psychology and what do psychologists study?

# 2.7 Ways the mind works

## Words in context

*Read the following passages and do the exercises.*

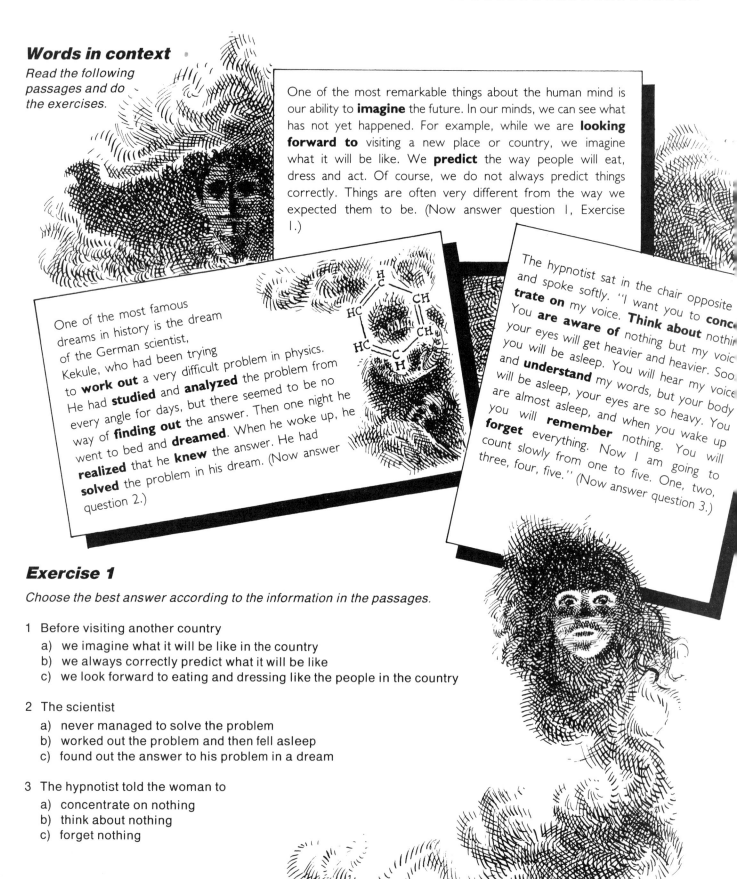

One of the most remarkable things about the human mind is our ability to **imagine** the future. In our minds, we can see what has not yet happened. For example, while we are **looking forward to** visiting a new place or country, we imagine what it will be like. We **predict** the way people will eat, dress and act. Of course, we do not always predict things correctly. Things are often very different from the way we expected them to be. (Now answer question 1, Exercise 1.)

One of the most famous dreams in history is the dream of the German scientist, Kekule, who had been trying to **work out** a very difficult problem in physics. He had **studied** and **analyzed** the problem from every angle for days, but there seemed to be no way of **finding out** the answer. Then one night he went to bed and **dreamed**. When he woke up, he **realized** that he **knew** the answer. He had **solved** the problem in his dream. (Now answer question 2.)

The hypnotist sat in the chair opposite and spoke softly. "I want you to conce **trate on** my voice. **Think about** nothin You **are aware of** nothing but my voic your eyes will get heavier and heavier. Soo you will be asleep. You will hear my voice and **understand** my words, but your body will be asleep, your eyes are so heavy. You are almost asleep, and when you wake up you will **remember** nothing. You will **forget** everything. Now I am going to count slowly from one to five. One, two, three, four, five." (Now answer question 3.)

## Exercise 1

*Choose the best answer according to the information in the passages.*

1 Before visiting another country
   a) we imagine what it will be like in the country
   b) we always correctly predict what it will be like
   c) we look forward to eating and dressing like the people in the country

2 The scientist
   a) never managed to solve the problem
   b) worked out the problem and then fell asleep
   c) found out the answer to his problem in a dream

3 The hypnotist told the woman to
   a) concentrate on nothing
   b) think about nothing
   c) forget nothing

## Exercise 2

*Use prepositions to fill the blanks in these sentences.*

1 Pay attention _____ me. You don't look as if you are listening to

2 one word I'm saying. What are you dreaming _____?

3 My sister is really looking forward _____ her next birthday. She

4 found _____ that she is getting a new bicycle.

5 Are you aware _____ how much work I have to do?

6 It's very difficult to concentrate _____ it while you are singing.

7 He had been thinking _____ the problem for ages. Now, at last, he

8 had worked _____ the answer.

9 It happened so long ago. I'd forgotten _____ it.

## Dictionary work

*Change these verbs into nouns and use them to fill the blanks in the sentences, as in the example.*
*Do as many as you can and then check your answers in a dictionary.*

Example: to decide  He made a good ____*decision*____.

1  to analyze      – She gave an interesting _____ of the problem.

2  to study        – I've made a _____ of the local customs.

3  to solve        – Who is going to find a _____ to this problem?

4  to imagine      – The child had a very strong _____.

5  to remember     – She had no _____ of what had happened.

6  to know         – I have no _____ of the matter.

7  to concentrate  – He needed all his powers of _____.

8  to realize      – She was suddenly struck by the _____.

9  to predict      – His _____ was wrong. The other team won.

10 to understand   – He has no _____ of the problem.

## Think about

1 Do you think hypnosis works? Do you think you could be hypnotized?

2 Do you find it easy to:  a) remember things clearly   b) study for hours
   c) work out mathematical problems?

3 Have you ever visited a place and then found it very different from what you expected?
   In what ways?

# 2.8 Unusual states of mind

**Words in context**   *Read the following passage and do the exercises.*

Several hundred years ago, in the small town of Pisa in Italy, there lived an unusual man. His name was Galileo. Galileo was a professor of mathematics. He always dressed in **strange** clothes and used to walk around the town talking to himself. The people of Pisa were never quite sure whether Galileo was totally **crazy** or an amazing genius. He certainly had some very **peculiar** ideas.

One day Galileo gathered together some people from the town and asked them, "What do you think will happen if I take one heavy ball and one much lighter ball and drop them at the same time from the top of the Leaning Tower of Pisa? Which ball do you think will hit the ground first?" Everyone thought this was a very **odd** question. The answer was obvious. Every **sensible** person knew that the heavy ball would land first. When Galileo said that they would arrive at the same time, the people were sure that he was **out of his mind**. He dropped the two balls and they came down exactly together.

Next, Galileo made a powerful telescope and started to study the sky. It was then that he came up with the craziest idea of all. He told the people that the earth was moving very fast and that it was going around the sun. Now they were sure he was **insane**. No sensible, **rational** person could believe such **weird** and absurd things. If the earth were moving, people would not be able to stand up. And how could the earth be going around the sun? The sun was in the east every morning and in the west every evening. Every **reasonable** person knew that the sun must therefore be going around the earth.

This time everyone knew he could not possibly be **sane**. Galileo was put in prison for a long time because of his dangerous ideas, and he was only set free when he was ready to say that he had made a mistake.

## Exercise 1

*Decide whether these statements are true (T) or false (F) according to the passage.*

1 _____ Galileo was a mathematics student.

2 _____ Galileo wore unusual clothes.

3 _____ **Sometimes the people of Pisa thought that Galileo was insane.**

4 _____ Galileo dropped two very similar balls from the Tower of Pisa.

5 _____ Most people thought the balls would hit the ground at different times.

6 _____ The balls hit the ground at different times.

7 _____ Galileo bought a telescope to study the stars.

8 _____ When Galileo said the earth was moving, people thought he was insane.

9 _____ **When Galileo said the earth was going around the sun, people thought he was a very sane person.**

## Exercise 2

*Which of these words can be used to describe the types of people below?*

a) sensible  b) reasonable  c) peculiar  d) crazy  e) rational  f) strange  g) out of his or her mind  h) odd  i) insane

1  A person who has serious mental problems may be described as _____  _____  _____

2  A person who makes good decisions after thinking carefully may be described as _____  _____  _____

3  A person who acts a little differently from most other people may be described as _____  _____  _____

## Exercise 3

*Match each statement on the left with a response on the right.*

1 _____  We'll get married when we've saved enough money.

2 _____  She lost her job yesterday and won a lot of money today.

3 _____  He has green hair.

4 _____  It's sunny and raining at the same time.

5 _____  Take an umbrella. It may rain.

6 _____  She keeps talking to herself.

7 _____  Let's wear our pajamas to the party.

8 _____  They went swimming in 0 degree weather.

a)  What strange weather!

b)  That's a very peculiar idea.

c)  That's a very sensible suggestion.

d)  That seems like a very rational decision.

e)  That's insane!

f)  What a weird-looking person!

g)  What a crazy life!

h)  What an odd woman!

## Dictionary work

*Put these adjectives describing states of mind in the right columns.*
*Do as many as you can and then check your answers in a dictionary.*

giddy    drunk    puzzled    amazed    intoxicated    astonished    dizzy    confused

| after too much alcohol | when you can't understand | when you are very surprised | after turning around and around |
|---|---|---|---|
| _____ | _____ | _____ | _____ |
| _____ | _____ | _____ | _____ |

## Think about

1  What are common examples of mental problems?

2  What are some of the causes of mental illness?

3  What are the most common forms of treatment for mental problems?

# 2.9 Good guys and bad guys

**Words in context**  *Read the following passage and do the exercises.*

**ean** Scarface Billy rode into Dodge City late one night. He was the most **ruthless** cowboy in the wild, wild West and many a man, woman and child had met their death from his smoking gun. He was a **cruel** man, who enjoyed hurting people. He was a **selfish** and **greedy** man, who would take the money from a blind man's plate. He was a **dishonest** man, who would lie to his own mother.

Billy rode up to the Lucky Horse Saloon and went in. The room went quiet as he walked up to the bar where Goodtime Lil was serving the drinks. ''Hi, Lil. Give me a whiskey,'' he said. ''Make it a bottle of whiskey.''

Goodtime Lil was Billy's girl. She was a **vain** girl, always looking at herself in mirrors and thinking how fine she looked. Because she was Billy's girl, she was a little **proud**, and thought she was more important than other people. But she was basically **good** and **kind**. She was always **sympathetic** when the customers told her their problems. And sometimes she was even **generous** and bought them a drink or two.

Meanwhile back at the Sheriff's office, a little boy came running in. ''Come quick,'' he said to the Sheriff. ''Mean Scarface Billy is back in town. He's over in the saloon right now.''

Sheriff Parker was the new Sheriff. He was young, brave and **honest**. He was also **sincere** in his wish to be **helpful** to the people of Dodge City, so he took his gun and went off to the saloon.

The Sheriff walked into the saloon holding his gun. ''Mean Scarface Billy,'' he called. ''I'm the new Sheriff around here. Put down your gun. You're coming with me.''

Billy laughed. ''You young fool,'' he said. And as he spoke he grabbed a young girl who was near him and held her in front of him. ''You'd better be careful, Sheriff. If you try to kill me, you may kill this **nice** innocent young girl.''

Then Mean Billy felt a piece of cold metal in the back of his neck. It was the gun of Goodtime Lil. ''I'm sorry, honey,'' she said, ''but this is the end for you and me. I've found a good man. I've found an **unselfish** man who thinks about other people before himself. As for you and me, we're finished.''

Sheriff Parker looked across at Lil. ''Thanks, baby,'' he said. ''I guess I'm your man now . . .''

## Exercise 1

*Put these pictures in the right order according to the passage.*

## Exercise 2

Which of these words are positive and which are negative?
Put a (+) sign next to the positive words and a (−) sign next to the negative words.

| | | | |
|---|---|---|---|
| 1 nice ( ) | 2 sympathetic ( ) | 3 cruel ( ) | 4 ruthless ( ) |
| 5 selfish ( ) | 6 kind ( ) | 7 mean ( ) | 8 honest ( ) |
| 9 generous ( ) | 10 helpful ( ) | 11 vain ( ) | 12 sincere ( ) |

## Exercise 3

Use these words to fill the blanks in the passage.

---

a) sincere   b) honest   c) cruel   d) nice   e) selfish   f) sympathetic   g) helpful   h) generous

---

Bob Twoface is a very successful business man. The people he works with don't like him very much because

he is very (1_____). He only does what he wants to do and never thinks about anyone else.

They also think that he is not an (2_____) man. They think he doesn't always tell the truth.

At home, he is a very different person. He is (3_____) in the house and the backyard. He has a very (4_____) ear

and will listen carefully to your problems. He is (5_____) to his dogs and cats and has certainly never been

(6_____) to them. He is also very (7_____) and last year he gave ten thousand dollars to the poor.

People who know Bob both at home and at work often ask themselves: "Which is the real Bob Twoface?

How (8_____) is he?"

## Dictionary work

Find the phrase in the first column that best completes the sentence in the second column.
You may have to look up the words in dark print in a dictionary, but answer as many as you can first.

| | |
|---|---|
| 1 _____ People who are honest | a) **share** things with others. |
| 2 _____ People who are cruel | b) **lie**. |
| 3 _____ People who are proud | c) never **cheat**. |
| 4 _____ People who are generous | d) **care about** others. |
| 5 _____ People who are sympathetic | e) **grab** more than others. |
| 6 _____ People who are dishonest | f) **admire** themselves. |
| 7 _____ People who are greedy | g) **hurt** other people. |

## Think about

1 How would you describe a "good" person?
2 Are there times when it is right to be dishonest and tell a lie?
3 How generous are you? Do you give money if a person asks you for money in the street?
4 Which are more helpful and unselfish:   a) city people or country people   b) young or old   c) rich or poor?

# 2.10 National characteristics

▪▪▪▪▪▪▪▪▪▪▪▪▪▪▪▪▪▪▪▪▪▪▪▪▪▪▪▪▪▪▪▪▪▪▪▪▪▪▪▪▪▪▪▪▪▪▪▪▪▪

Dear Frank,

Hi! How are you getting along in the States? I'm having a wonderful time here in England with your family and friends. Everyone is so <u>friendly</u> and <u>hospitable</u>. They all welcome me into their homes and treat me as one of the family.

I've been very surprised by English people. I thought they would all be very conservative and <u>traditional</u>. Instead I've found them very open to new ideas. I also thought English people would be rather <u>shy</u>. But most people seem very <u>outgoing</u> and <u>self-confident</u>, almost as much as Americans. I find the English very <u>tolerant</u> too. Nobody here seems to mind very much how you dress or what you say. Of course, there are some <u>narrow-minded</u> people too. But I don't think there are as many as there are back home in the States.

I often think of you in my home and what you must be thinking about Americans. I imagine you think we're too <u>hard-working</u> and too <u>materialistic</u>. I never realized how much Americans talk about money, until I came to Britain. And you probably also think that Americans are very <u>rude</u> compared with the British. I don't think we're really so rude, it's just that we sometimes forget to use all those <u>polite</u> phrases like "do you mind" and "could I" and "may I."

One difference I have noticed is that the British don't seem as <u>optimistic</u> as Americans. In America we always think we can change things and make them better. But I get the feeling that the British have a rather <u>pessimistic</u> view of life.

I'm feeling <u>lazy</u>, so that's all I'm going to write now. I look forward to hearing your impressions of the U.S.

Yours,
Dave

## Words in context

*Read the following letter and do the exercises.*

This is a letter from Dave. Dave is an American exchange student in Great Britain, who is living in Frank's home, while Frank is staying in the U.S. with Dave's family.

## Exercise 1

*According to Dave, do these words best describe British people (B) or American people (A)?*

1 rude _____    2 materialistic _____    3 hard-working _____

4 tolerant _____    5 self-confident _____    6 optimistic _____

## Exercise 2

Find the words in Dave's letter which mean the following:

a) treating someone as one of the family _____

b) not minding how other people dress and talk _____

c) not open to new ideas _____

d) sure of yourself _____

e) using words like "please" and "may I" _____

f) thinking you can make things better _____

## Exercise 3

Find five pairs of words which are opposite in meaning and use them to fill in the chart.

| |
|---|
| _____ and _____ |
| _____ and _____ |
| _____ and _____ |
| _____ and _____ |
| _____ and _____ |

| | |
|---|---|
| tolerant | polite |
| optimistic | shy |
| lazy | narrow-minded |
| rude | outgoing |
| pessimistic | hard-working |

## Just for fun

Think of a nationality (for example English, American, or your own nationality).
Put these characteristics in order from most typical (1) to least typical (8) of that nationality.

polite _____        friendly _____

shy _____        tolerant _____

traditional _____        hard-working _____

hospitable _____        materialistic _____

Now compare your answers with other people's and see whether they agree with you.

## Think about

1 What characteristics do people from other countries think people from your country have?
  Do you think they are right or wrong?

2 Do you sometimes feel shy? In what situations?

3 In what ways do you think your parents' generation is different from your generation?

4 Are you optimistic or pessimistic about the future? Why?

# Vocabulary review

## 2 The inner self (Units 2.6–2.10)

### 2.6 Intelligence

bright
brilliant
clever
fool
foolish
genius
idiot
intelligent
silly
slow
smart
stupid
unintelligent

### 2.7 Ways the mind works

analyze
be aware of
concentrate on
decide
dream
find out
forget
imagine
know
look forward to
pay attention to
predict
realize
remember
solve
study
think about
understand
work out

### 2.8 Unusual states of mind

amazed
astonished
confused
crazy
dizzy
drunk
giddy
insane
intoxicated
odd
out of one's mind
peculiar
puzzled
rational
reasonable
sane
sensible
strange
weird

### 2.9 Good guys and bad guys

admire
care about
cheat
cruel
dishonest
generous
good
grab
greedy
helpful
honest
hurt
kind
lie
mean
nice
proud
ruthless
selfish
share
sincere
sympathetic
unselfish
vain

### 2.10 National characteristics

friendly
hard-working
hospitable
lazy
materialistic
narrow-minded
optimistic
outgoing
pessimistic
polite
rude
self-confident
shy
tolerant
traditional

# Test yourself 4

Use the words from the **Vocabulary review** to help you fill the blanks in these sentences. In some cases you have been given the last letter of the word. More than one answer may be possible, but there is usually one best answer.

1 She's so _____, she never says "please" or "thank you."

2 "Do you _____ how old I am?"
  "I think you're about twenty-two years old."

3 The music is so loud I can't _____e on my homework.

4 Do you think it is really _____t to lie about your age?

5 You're so _____. You shouldn't care so much about money.

6 At first, I didn't know why his hand looked _____e, but then I

7 _____d that he had six fingers.

8 "I think people who don't wear seat belts in a car are very _____h."

9 "I agree. Wearing a seat belt is a very _____e thing to do."

10 I must be an_____t. I'm sure this problem is very simple, but I just can't work out the answer.

11 During the examination the teacher saw that one of the students was _____. She was looking at another student's answers.

12 "This mathematics problem is so difficult. I don't think I'll ever _____ it."

13 "Oh, that's why you have such a _____d look on your face."

14 I'm extremely _____c. I don't think there will ever be another world war.

15 "My little brother is very _____. He ate all the ice cream."

16 "What a _____h boy! He could have left some for us."

17 In many countries it is _____l for a woman to wear white clothes on her wedding day.

18 Often the people who have the most money are the least _____s.

19 "You're so _____. You get up late, go to bed early, and never do any work in the house."

20 "That's because, in my opinion, it's _____d to work too hard."

21 Don't you agree that Mozart was a _____s? He was writing music by the age of four!

22 "Can you _____ what is going to happen tomorrow?"

23 "I'm _____t but I'm not a genius. Nobody can be sure about the future."

24 Some people who don't like to talk very much may not be _____, they may just be quiet people.

25 I had a very _____r dream last night.

# 3 The world around us

## 3.1 Small towns and big cities

**Words in context**  *Read the following passage and do the exercises.*

Today, people all over the world are moving out of small **towns** in the **country** to go and live in big, noisy **cities**. They are moving from the peaceful **hills, mountains, fields, rivers** and **streams** of the **countryside** to the busy world of streets, buildings, traffic and crowds. This movement from **rural areas** to **urban areas** has been going on for over two hundred years.

In many countries, the main reason people come to live in towns and cities is work. After one or two large **factories** or businesses have been built in or near a city, people come to find work, and soon an **industrial area** begins to grow. There is usually a **residential area** nearby, where the factory workers can live. The families of these workers need **schools**, hospitals and **stores**, so more people come to live in the area to provide these services—and so a city grows.

In every major city in the world, there is a **business district** where the big companies have their main offices. In the United States, this is usually in the **downtown** area of the city. It is here that you can see the huge **skyscrapers** containing many floors of offices. The people who work here often travel a long

way to work each day. Many of them live in the **suburbs** of the city, far away from the industrial and business areas. Some suburbs are very pleasant, with nice houses and big **yards**. There are usually **parks** for children to play in and large **department stores** in **shopping malls** where you can buy all you need.

But what is the future of the big cities? Will they continue to get bigger and bigger? Maybe not. Some major cities have actually become smaller in the last ten years, and it is quite possible that one day we will see people moving out of the major cities and back into smaller towns.

### Exercise 1

*Decide whether these statements are true (T) or false (F) according to the passage.*

1 _____ Many people from small towns go to live in big cities.

2 _____ Urban areas contain mainly hills, mountains, rivers and streams.

3 _____ Many people go to live in urban areas to find work.

4 _____ Factories are built inside residential areas.

5 _____ Business districts are usually in the downtown area of the city.

6 _____ Workers often live in skyscrapers in the suburbs.

7 _____ The suburbs of a city usually contain more trees and parks than the downtown areas.

8 _____ The movement from country to city will definitely continue in the future.

## Exercise 2

Look at the picture and find these areas.

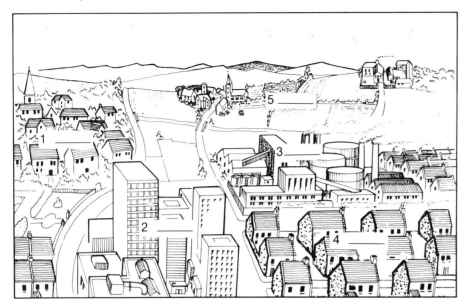

a) the industrial area

b) the suburbs

c) the residential area

d) the business district

e) the rural area

## Exercise 3

Look at these pairs of items. Decide which is larger in size and put an X next to it.

1 _____ hill    X mountain

2 _____ town    _____ city

3 _____ city    _____ business district

4 _____ field    _____ countryside

5 _____ urban area    _____ downtown area

6 _____ skyscraper    _____ house

7 _____ river    _____ stream

8 _____ park    _____ yard

9 _____ shopping mall _____ department store

10 _____ factory    _____ industrial area

11 _____ rural area    _____ farm

12 _____ house    _____ residential area

## Dictionary work

Look at this list of buildings. Write (H) next to those buildings which can be people's homes.
Do as many as you can and then check your answers in a dictionary.

1 _____ schools    2 _____ farms    3 _____ mansions

4 _____ castles    5 _____ banks    6 _____ apartments

7 _____ museums    8 _____ palaces    9 _____ hotels

10 _____ theaters    11 _____ ranches    12 _____ churches

13 _____ cathedrals    14 _____ cabins    15 _____ garages

## Think about

1 Do you live in a rural area, a town, or a big city?
2 What are the advantages and disadvantages of living in a big city?
3 Where would you like to live and why?

# 3.2 The world of plants

**Words in context** *Read the following passages and do the exercises.*

Without **plants**, people could not live. We eat plants. We breathe the oxygen that plants produce. And we need plants for another, very different reason: we need them for their beauty.

Imagine a world with no plants. Imagine no **flowers** with their sweet smells, their beautiful colors and their lovely shapes. Imagine, when the wind blows, not being able to hear the **leaves** in the **trees** or watch the **branches** swing from side to side. Imagine not being able to see the **buds** on the trees open and turn to colorful **blossoms**.

Everywhere people need the beauty of plants. That is why even in big modern cities, we have parks full of trees, **bushes** and flowers. That is why architects always try to design houses with room for some **grass** and a yard. That is why in every city apartment you are sure to find some green houseplants growing in **pots**, or freshly cut flowers in a **vase** of water. (Now answer questions 1, 2 and 3 in Exercise 1.)

Do you talk to your plants? Do you give them love and attention? According to Peter Tompkins and Christopher Bird, authors of a book called *The Secret Life of Plants* * you should talk to them and give them love.

Tompkins and Bird describe an experiment in which two **seeds** were planted in different places. While the plants were growing, one plant was given love and positive ideas. The other plant was given only negative ideas. After six months, the loved plant was bigger. Under the ground, it had more and longer **roots**; above the ground, it had a thicker **stem** and more leaves.

So be careful when you are talking in front of your plants. They may be listening to you! (Now answer questions 4, 5 and 6.)

*published by Penguin

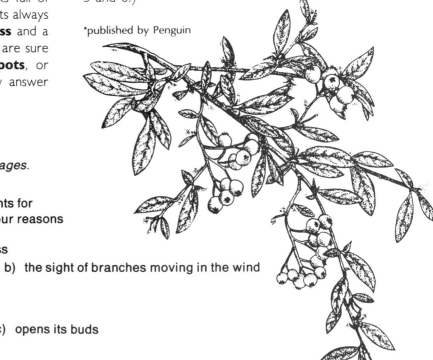

## Exercise 1

*Choose the best answer according to the passages.*

1 According to the first passage, we need plants for
   a) two reasons   b) three reasons   c) four reasons

2 If there were no plants, the writer would miss
   a) the smells, colors and shapes of trees   b) the sight of branches moving in the wind
   c) the sound of flowers blowing in the wind

3 Just before it blossoms, a tree
   a) loses its leaves   b) closes its buds   c) opens its buds

4 According to Tompkins and Bird, plants
   a) love to talk   b) love to be loved   c) love to love

5 In the experiment, the two plants were
   a) talked to in two different ways   b) planted in the same place   c) both given love and attention

6 At the end of six months
   a) the plants were the same size   b) one plant had longer roots than the other
   c) one plant had longer roots, the other plant had a thicker stem

## Exercise 2

Match these words with the pictures.

| a) tree | b) vase | c) seed | d) stem | e) flower | f) branch |
|---------|---------|---------|---------|-----------|-----------|
| g) bud | h) roots | i) leaf | j) blossom | k) bush | l) pot |

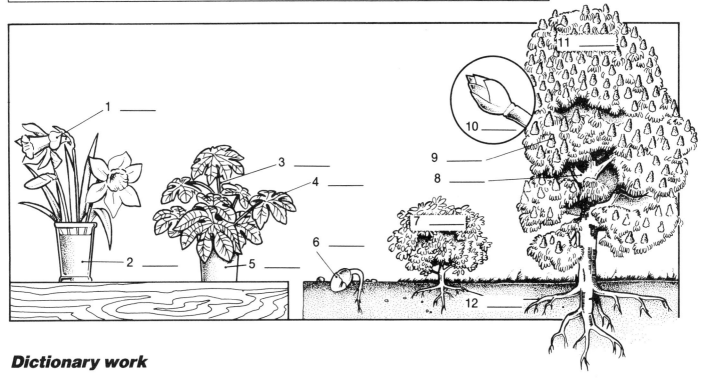

## Dictionary work

Match the definitions with the words. Do as many as you can and then check your answers in a dictionary.

1 _____ dried grass which is used to feed cows and horses      a) weed

2 _____ a type of grass grown to make bread      b) seaweed

3 _____ a thick forest in a hot country      c) palm

4 _____ a plant that is often used in cooking or medicine      d) wheat

5 _____ a tree that grows a lot in hot countries      e) rose

6 _____ an unwanted wild plant      f) herb

7 _____ a tree whose wood is often used for furniture      g) hay

8 _____ a plant that grows near or in the ocean      h) jungle

9 _____ a beautiful flower      i) oak

## Think about

1 What do you think of the idea that you should talk to your plants and give them love?
2 In English, we say someone has "a green thumb" if plants grow well for them.
  Do you enjoy gardening and taking care of plants? Do you have a green thumb?
3 When do people give each other flowers in your country?

# 3.3 The animal kingdom

**Words in context** *Read the following passages and do the exercises.*

What is an animal? For many people, an animal has four legs, a head at the front and a **tail** at the back. There are, in fact, many different kinds of animals. Some are so small that you cannot see them with the human eye. Some have no head, no mouth, no legs. Some live in the ocean. Some can't fly. They come in thousands of different shapes, sizes and colors.

Here is a page from a biology textbook which shows how different animals can be.

**Insects.** One of the largest groups of animals is the insect group. These animals have six legs and three parts to their bodies. Many insects cause humans problems. Some carry diseases. Others are a problem because they eat the food that farmers grow. But there are insects, like **bees** and **butterflies**, that we need because they help flowers and fruit to grow.

**Birds.** Like many of the insects, birds have **wings** and can fly. There are many different types of birds. Some eat fish and are happy living near rivers or the ocean. Others like to live in the countryside or near towns in flocks of many hundreds and eat mostly insects, and there are birds which like to live alone high in the mountains. These birds, like the mountain **eagle**, eat meat with their strong sharp **beaks**. They also have sharp **claws** on their feet, which are perfect for hunting and killing.

**Fish** and **reptiles**. Fish and reptiles are cold-blooded animals. Fish live in the ocean, but reptiles usually live on the land. Reptiles are probably the least popular animals. They include the long thin **snakes** that many people are afraid of. However, some people keep snakes in their homes as pets!

**Mammals.** Like birds, mammals are warm-blooded, and just as all birds have **feathers**, all mammals have hair on their bodies. Sometimes you can hardly see the hair. Sometimes the hair is very thick, and then it is called **fur**. There are several different groups of mammals. There are the cats, which include **lions** and **tigers**; there are animals with large front teeth, which include **mice** and **rats**; there are the sea mammals, which include the **whale**, the largest animal in the world. Then there are animals which have two arms and can walk on two legs like **monkeys** and, of course, humans.

Now, how would you answer the question: what is an animal?

## Exercise 1

*Decide whether these statements are true (T) or false (F) according to the passages.*

1 _____ All animals have four legs.

2 _____ All insects have three parts to their bodies.

3 _____ All insects cause people problems.

4 _____ All birds and insects have wings.

5 _____ Some birds eat fish.

6 _____ Some fish live on the land.

7 _____ All reptiles live on the land.

8 _____ All mammals live on the land.

9 _____ All mammals have hair on their skin.

10 _____ A whale is a mammal.

## Exercise 2

*Match the names of the animals with the pictures.*

a) a bee    b) a butterfly    c) a rat    d) a whale    e) a lion    f) an eagle    g) a snake    h) a monkey

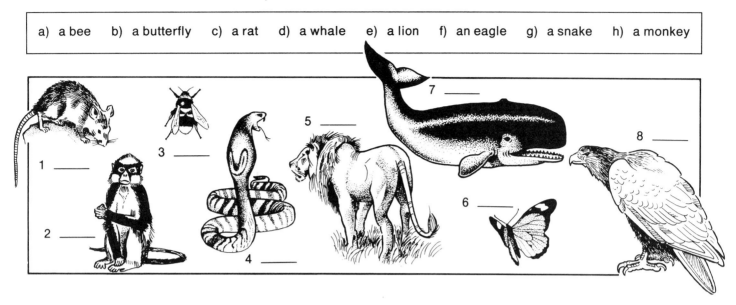

## Exercise 3

*Match the parts of animals on the left with the definitions on the right.*

1 _____ wing          a) a bird's mouth

2 _____ fur           b) a part which sticks out at the end of an animal's body

3 _____ tail          c) thick hair on the bodies of some mammals

4 _____ feather       d) one of the sharp, hard points on the feet of some birds and mammals

5 _____ beak          e) part of an animal which is used for flying

6 _____ claw          g) one of many parts of the covering that grows on a bird's body

## Dictionary work

*Put each animal in one of the four columns. Do as many as you can and then check your answers in a dictionary.*

| shark | crocodile | parrot | owl | wasp | mouse |
|-------|-----------|--------|-----|------|-------|
| goat  | seagull   | fly    | lizard | beetle | tiger |

| insects | birds | fish and reptiles | mammals |
|---------|-------|-------------------|---------|
|         |       |                   |         |
|         |       |                   |         |
|         |       |                   |         |

## Think about

1 Do people in your country keep pets? If so, which are the most common?

2 What unusual pets do some people keep?

3 What dangerous animals do you have in your country?

4 Some people think it is wrong to keep animals in zoos. Do you agree?

# 3.4 Weather

**Words in context**  *Read the following dialogue and do the exercises.*

A young Californian and an Englishman have just met on a ski lift in the Swiss Alps.

MIKE:   So, you're from **sunny** California. Tell me, is it really **hot** in southern California all year round?

DAVID:  No, it can get **cold**. But never **freezing** cold. It never **snows** in Los Angeles for example. But it's **chilly** in winter, especially in the evenings.

MIKE:   Does it ever **rain**?

DAVID:  Not much. But in January and February we sometimes get really heavy **rainstorms** that last all day.

MIKE:   And what's the summer like?

DAVID:  It can be **boiling hot** in the summer. Too warm for me. In Los Angeles, it gets **smoggy** too. Your eyes hurt and you can't see the sun.

MIKE:   How awful!

DAVID:  Yes, it is. But what about English weather? Is it true that London is very foggy?

MIKE:   No. People always think that. You see it all the time in the movies, but actually London hasn't had any thick **fogs** since the 1950s. The weather in England is bad though.

DAVID:  Yes, I've heard that, but how bad is it?

MIKE:   Well, for one thing, it never gets really hot, even in the summer. And for another, it rains a lot. Sometimes you can't even see the rain. It's just a light **drizzle**, but if you're outside you get soaking wet.

DAVID:  Sort of like an ocean **mist**?

MIKE:   Yeah, that's right. Of course the weather in England is also very **changeable**. You know, one minute the sun is shining. Then the sun goes behind a cloud and it gets all dark and **cloudy**. Then there'll be a terrible **storm** with loud **thunder** and flashes of **lightning**. Then suddenly the sun is out again and it's lovely and bright. But just when you think it's safe to go out, along comes a quick **shower** and it's **pouring** rain again.

DAVID:  Sounds terrible. What do you think of the weather here?

MIKE:   It's great. I love the snow. As long as there's no **wind** it's all right. Even a light **breeze** is unpleasant in the snow, don't you think?

DAVID:  Yeah, I guess you're right. But every now and then we need a heavy **snowstorm** like that **blizzard** last night, so we can get some nice fresh snow to ski on. Well, here we are. Nice talking to you. Enjoy the skiing.

## Exercise 1

*Look at the descriptions of weather and decide whether they are true of Los Angeles and/or London weather, according to the dialogue. Put an X in the right boxes.*

|  | rains often | only chilly in winter | changeable | drizzles | sudden showers | smoggy | never snows | can be boiling |
|---|---|---|---|---|---|---|---|---|
| **London** |  |  |  |  |  |  |  |  |
| **Los Angeles** |  |  |  |  |  |  |  |  |

## Exercise 2

Each of these pairs of words has a similar meaning, but one word in each pair is stronger.
Put an X against the word with the stronger meaning, as in the example.

1 ☒ fog ____ mist    2 ____ cold ____ freezing    3 ____ chilly ____ cold

4 ____ raining ____ pouring    5 ____ breeze ____ wind    6 ____ snowstorm ____ blizzard

## Exercise 3

Look at this weather map of Western Europe. Then fill in the blanks in the sentences with the correct words.

| a) sunny  b) thunder  c) windy  d) showers  e) lightning  f) storms  g) rain  h) cloudy  i) hot |
| --- |

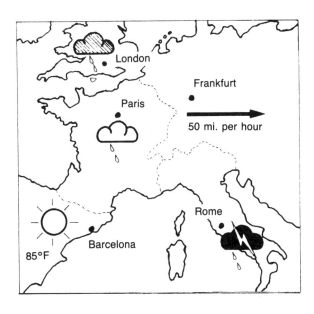

1 Paris will be partly _____

   with occasional _____

2 In London you can expect _____

   throughout the day.

3 Barcelona should be very _____

   and _____ all day.

4 It will be very _____ in Frankfurt.

5 You can expect to find _____

   and _____ in Rome during some

   heavy summer _____

## Just for fun

```
R  A  D  M  E  E  G  O  P  T
T  H  D  R  C  H  I  L  L  Y
H  I  A  R  I  A  N  G  A  R
U  S  S  E  A  Z  E  N  A  C
N  O  W  S  P  Z  Z  I  O  L
D  W  O  N  E  E  N  L  L  O
E  L  I  E  Z  K  D  I  E  U
R  E  R  E  E  C  H  O  L  D
T  B  W  O  N  S  O  B  O  B
O  R  L  P  O  U  R  I  N  G
```

There are nine words that describe
weather hidden in this square.
The words may be written forwards,
backwards, diagonally, up or down.
Can you find them?

## Think about

1 What is the weather like in your country?
2 Do you have seasons in your country? When are they? Which is your favorite and why?
3 What is the weather like right now? What has it been like for the last couple of days?
4 What sort of climate would you like to live in?

# 3.5 Energy sources

**Words in context**   *Read the following passages and do the exercises.*

**Coal.** It was coal that produced the **energy** to run the factories of the first big industrial countries, such as Great Britain and Germany. Coal miners worked long hard hours in cold dark **coal mines** to bring this black rock above ground. They called it black gold.

**Oil and gas.** Texas, Saudi Arabia, Kuwait and Venezuela: these are only a few of the places where oil has been found. Today, big oil companies still spend millions of dollars looking for oil, and when they find it, a new **oil well** is started and the company makes even more millions. Sometimes they don't find oil underneath the earth. They find gas. But gas, too, can be used for energy. It is a good energy source for heating and cooking.

**Nuclear** or **atomic** energy. It is incredible to think that from the nucleus of the atom—one of the smallest things in the world—can come enormous amounts of energy. This energy, which is called nuclear or atomic energy, can either be controlled in **nuclear power stations** to create electricity for millions of homes, or it can be used in war to destroy millions of homes.

**Hydroelectric power.** Water from fast-running rivers is another source of energy. By building large **dams** to control the water, millions of kilowatts of power can be produced. Countries get most of their electricity from hydroelectric power.

**Solar** and **wind energy**. In the future, much of our energy may come from the sun. In some countries, **solar collectors** on the roof can already create enough **solar power** to heat and provide electricity for a house in both winter and summer. One day we may also see small **windmills** on every roof. Even a small wind can provide enough **power** to run lights and most electrical machines in the home.

## Exercise 1

*Change the words in dark print to make the sentences true, according to the information in the passages.*

1 The color of a piece of coal is **gold**.   _____

2 Sweden and Norway produce a great deal of **solar energy**.   _____

3 There are many **water** wells in Saudi Arabia.   _____

4 Another word for atomic energy is **hydroelectric** energy.   _____

5 When oil companies look for oil they sometimes find **coal** instead.   _____

6 **Solar collectors** can be used to catch the power of the wind.   _____

7 A **nuclear power station** is used to stop water in fast-running rivers.   _____

8 **Hydroelectric** power can be used in war to kill millions of people.   _____

# Exercise 2

*Match the words with the pictures.*

| | | | | |
|---|---|---|---|---|
| a) oil | b) nuclear power station | c) coal | d) windmill | e) solar collectors |
| f) coal mine | g) dam | h) wind power | i) gas | j) oil well |

## Just for fun

*How cheap, clean, safe, and abundant (i.e., there is a lot of it in the world) do you think each energy source is? Use the scale next to the chart and rate the energy sources.*

| | cheap | clean | safe | abundant |
|---|---|---|---|---|
| coal | | | | |
| oil | | | | |
| solar | | | | |
| nuclear | | | | |

| not at all | | fairly | | very |
|---|---|---|---|---|
| 1 | 2 | 3 | 4 | 5 |

## Think about

1 Which sources of energy are used in your country?

2 Are you for or against nuclear energy? Why?

3 Can you think of some ways of saving energy?

4 What other sources of energy do you know of? Make a list.

# Vocabulary review

## 3 The world around us (Units 3.1–3.5)

### 3.1 Small towns, big cities

area
apartment
bank
bungalow
business district
castle
cathedral
church
city
cottage
country
countryside
department store
downtown
factory
farm
field
garage
garden
hill
hotel
industrial
mansion
mountain
museum
palace
park
residential
river
rural
school
shopping mall
skyscraper
store
stream
suburb
theater
town
urban
village
yard

### 3.2 The world of plants

blossom
branch
bud
bush
flower
grass
hay
herb
jungle
leaf
oak
palm
plant
pot
root
rose
seaweed
seed
stem
tree
vase
weed
wheat

### 3.3 The animal kingdom

beak
bee
beetle
bird
butterfly
cat
claw
crocodile
eagle
feather
fish
fly
fur
goat
insect
lion
lizard
mammal
monkey
mouse
owl
parrot
rat
reptile
seagull
shark
snake
tail
tiger
wasp
whale
wing

### 3.4 Weather

blizzard
boiling
breeze
changeable
chilly
cloudy
cold
drizzle
fog
freezing
hot
lightning
mist
pouring
rain
rainstorm
shower
smoggy
snow
snowstorm
storm
sunny
thunder
wind

### 3.5 Energy sources

atomic energy
coal
coal mine
dam
energy
gas
hydroelectric power
nuclear energy
nuclear power station
oil
oil well
power
solar collector
solar power
windmill
wind power

# *Test yourself 5*

▪▪▪▪▪▪▪▪▪▪▪▪▪▪▪▪▪▪▪▪▪▪▪▪▪▪▪▪▪▪▪▪▪▪▪▪▪▪▪▪▪▪▪▪▪▪▪▪▪▪

Use the words from the **Vocabulary review** to help you fill the blanks in these sentences. In some cases you have been given the last letter of the word. More than one answer may be possible, but there is usually one best answer.

1  The largest animal is the _____. It lives in the ocean, but it is not a fish.

2  It's a _____l.

3  Can you see the _____y in that tree? Look it's on the third

4  _____h on the right.

5  I work downtown, but I live in the _____. It takes me
over an hour to get to work every day.

6  Some people don't like gardening because you have to pull up all the _____ around the

7  flower beds, and of course you have to keep cutting the _____s. It's a lot of work.

8  My uncle raises cattle on a big _____ in Texas.

9  Many people think that _____r energy is too dangerous. They think

10  that we should continue to use _____l and also try to find other new sources of energy.

"What kind of tree is this?"

11  "It's a lemon tree. Don't the _____s smell wonderful?"

12  New York is famous for its _____s.

13  These trees do not lose their _____ in winter.

14  Cats like to chase birds, mice and _____s.

15  One day while I was walking in the _____e near my town,

16  there was a big storm. A tree near me was struck by _____g.

17  It is dangerous to walk in the jungle. They say there are poisonous _____.

18  The _____ is terrible. I can't see anything. I'll have to stop driving.

19  Some people don't like living in cities and prefer to live in the _____ where life is quieter.

"Why is the ground wet?"

20  "While you were sleeping there was a quick _____r."

21  I don't think there is enough _____r in this wind to turn this old

22  _____l.

23  It's _____g today. I'm going to have to wear my warmest clothes when

24  I go out . I hope the snowstorm doesn't turn into a _____d.

25  The weatherman on television said it was going to be _____y in the morning,
but that the sun would come out in the afternoon.

# 3.6  Traveling by air

**Words in context**  *Read the following passage and do the exercises.*

I knew it was going to be a bad day when, on the way to the airport, the taxi driver told me he was lost.

I had **booked** my **flight** over the telephone, so when we finally arrived, I had to rush to the **reservations desk** to pay for my **ticket**. The woman at the desk told me that my name was not on the **passenger** list. It took fifteen minutes for her to realize that she had spelled my name incorrectly. She gave me my ticket and told me I'd better **check in** my **luggage** quickly or I'd **miss** my flight.

I was the last person to **get on** the plane.

I found my seat and discovered that I was sitting next to a four-year-old boy who had a cold. I sat down and wondered if anything else could go wrong.

I hate flying, especially take-off, but the plane **took off** and everything seemed to be all right. Then, a few minutes later, there was a funny noise and everything started to shake. I looked out of the window and—oh my goodness—there was smoke coming out of the wing. All I could think of was "The **engine** is on fire. We're going to crash. I'm too young to die."

Almost immediately, the captain spoke to us in a very calm voice, "Ladies and gentlemen. This is your captain speaking. We are having a slight technical problem with one of our engines. There is absolutely no need to panic. We will have to return to the airport. Please remain seated and keep your **seat belts** fastened."

Well you can imagine how frightened I was, but the **crew** was fantastic. The **flight attendants** were really calm and told us not to worry. One of them told me to relax and said that everything would be all right.

A few minutes later, we were coming in to **land**. The **pilot** made a perfect landing on the **runway**. It was over. We were safe.

That day, I decided not to fly again. I **caught** another taxi and went home. But as I closed the front door, I looked down. Somehow I had picked up the wrong **suitcase**.

## Exercise 1

*Put these events in the right order, according to the passage.*

a) She paid for her ticket.

b) The engine caught fire.

c) The plane landed.

d) The plane took off.

e) She picked up the wrong suitcase.

f) The reservations clerk couldn't find her name.

g) The taxi driver got lost.

h) She went home.

i) The flight attendants told people to be calm.

j) She booked the flight.

k) She left home.

l) She checked in her luggage.

1 _____   2 _____   3 _____   4 _____   5 _____   6 _____

7 _____   8 _____   9 _____   10 _____   11 _____   12 _____

## Exercise 2

*Find the words in the story which mean the following and write them in the blanks.*

1 The desk where you can get your ticket if you have made a reservation _____

2 The part of an airport where a plane takes off and lands _____

3 A group of peope who work on a plane _____

4 A person who flies a plane _____

5 A person who is traveling on a plane _____

6 A person who takes care of the people who are traveling on a plane _____

## Exercise 3

*Match the beginning of the sentence with the end.*

| | | |
|---|---|---|
| 1 _____ I checked in | a) | their flight. |
| 2 _____ She got on | b) | my ticket. |
| 3 _____ The travel agent made | c) | their seat belts. |
| 4 _____ The pilot landed on | d) | the plane. |
| 5 _____ She caught | e) | my luggage. |
| 6 _____ They almost missed | f) | a taxi. |
| 7 _____ The passengers fastened | g) | the runway. |
| 8 _____ I booked | h) | my reservation. |
| 9 _____ The crew was | i) | her suitcase. |
| 10 _____ She picked up | j) | very calm. |

## Just for fun

*Imagine you are traveling 1500 miles. You can go by car, train, plane, bus or boat.*
*Fill in the chart with the form of transportation you think would be cheapest, most uncomfortable,*
*slowest, etc., when traveling alone and with a friend. Compare and discuss your answers with a friend.*

| | cheapest | slowest | most uncomfortable | most interesting |
|---|---|---|---|---|
| **alone** | | | | |
| **with a friend** | | | | |

## Think about

1 Are you afraid of flying? Which form of transportation do you believe is safest and which is most dangerous?
2 Have you ever had a bad experience while traveling? What happened?
3 What are the advantages and disadvantages of traveling alone?

# 3.7 Driving a car

**Words in context**  *Read the following passage and do the exercises.*

Here is a list of good driving habits.

1   It is dangerous to **drive** too close to the car in front of you. If it stops suddenly, you may not be able to **brake** in time and then you will **crash** into it.

2   **Pass** the car in front of you with great care. When you are absolutely sure that the road ahead is clear, change lanes, **accelerate** and overtake quickly.

3   The speed limit is for normal conditions. If the weather is bad, you should drive **under the speed limit**. Never drive **over the speed limit**.

4   Children get **run over** because they run out into the street without looking. When you see children playing, you should **slow down** and drive very carefully.

5   If you have to **park** on a hill, put the **emergency brake** on. Also, put the car in **gear** (not neutral) and turn the front **wheels** towards the side of the road.

6   Use your **rear-view mirror** frequently to see what the traffic is doing on the road behind you. Good drivers look in their rear-view mirrors at least once every five seconds.

7   Keep your car in good condition. Check often to see whether you have enough oil in your engine, enough air in your **tires** and enough water in your radiator. Make sure all your lights (**headlights, taillights** and **turn signals**) are working. Only drive with brakes that are in good condition.

8   Always wear your **seat belt**. You do not want to go through the **windshield** if the car stops suddenly.

## Exercise 1

*Look at these pictures and write down the number of the safe driving rule that has been broken.*

a _____   b _____   c _____

d _____   e _____   f _____

## Exercise 2

*Name the parts of the car in these two pictures.*

| | | | | |
|---|---|---|---|---|
| a) windshield | b) wheel | c) tire | d) headlight | e) emergency brake |
| f) gear shift | g) rear-view mirror | h) seat belt | i) turn signal | |

 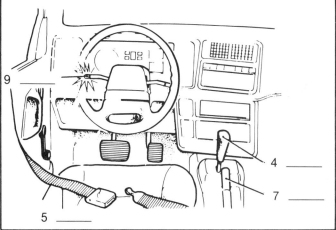

## Dictionary work

*Match the driving action with its definition. Do as many as you can and then check your answers in a dictionary.*

1 _____ accelerate

2 _____ pass

3 _____ drive over the speed limit

4 _____ park

5 _____ crash

6 _____ look in your rear-view mirror

7 _____ slow down

8 _____ run someone over

9 _____ brake

a) make your car go less fast

b) make your car go faster

c) make your car go too fast

d) knock a person down

e) go past the car in front

f) stop your car by the side of the road

g) hit another car, wall, tree, etc.

h) make your car stop

i) watch the traffic behind you

## Think about

1 At what age can people drive in your country? Can you drive?

2 What sort of car would you like to drive and why?

3 Do you have to wear seat belts in your country? Do you think this is a good law?

4 What happens to drivers who break the law in your country?

# 3.8 Noises

**Words in context**  *Read the following passage and do the exercises.*

Mrs. Carter was a rich woman who lived in a big house. She had a video security system, but on the night she was murdered, the camera was not working. Only the sounds were recorded. A group of detectives are now listening to the tape of the murder. This is what they can hear.

*A dog **barks**..,. the doorbell **rings** . . . a person **snores** . . . then a **knock** at the door . . . a **click** . . . a second click . . . the sound of drawers opening and closing . . . a cat **cries** . . . a **sneeze** . . . a **yawn** . . . the **creak** of a door . . . a **gasp** . . . a **scream** . . .a **shot** . . . the **crash** of glass breaking . . . **groaning** . . . the **bang** of the door . . . the **roar** of a car engine . . . the dog **growls**.*

Chief Detective Lee gets up and says. "OK. From the information on the tape, we have a good idea of what happened in the house. Let me explain. First, we hear the dog bark, but only for a couple of seconds. Then we hear someone ring the doorbell and knock on the door. But Mrs. Carter doesn't wake up. We can hear her snoring in the bedroom.

The person at the door (who we are almost certain is a man) probably thinks the house is empty. There is one click as he unlocks the front door. That's the first click. Then, almost immediately, he turns on the lights, and that's the second click on the tape. The man then walks straight over to Mrs. Carter's study, which is across from her bedroom, and starts opening and closing drawers. He is looking for something—maybe money.

At this point the cat starts crying and the man sneezes. Maybe he is allergic to cats. I think the sneeze must have woken Mrs. Carter up because you can hear her yawn sleepily. The next thing you hear is a creak, which is almost certainly Mrs. Carter slowly opening her bedroom door. She then sees the man in her study and he shoots her. There is a crash as Mrs. Carter falls to the ground, knocking over a vase of flowers. She does not die immediately, but groans in pain.

The man leaves the house quickly. He bangs the front door, gets into his car and drives away with a loud roar. The dog growls angrily.

Well, what do you think? Was Mrs. Carter killed by a man she knew or a stranger? I think we can tell from the tape, don't you?"

## Exercise 1

*Look at these pieces of information taken from the passage. Put an X next to the ones that make you think that the man knew Mrs. Carter.*

1 The dog barks for only a couple of seconds. _____

2 The man rings the doorbell and knocks on the door. _____

3 The man thinks the house is empty. _____

4 The man unlocks the door with one click. _____

5 Almost immediately the man turns on the lights. _____

6 He walks straight to the study and starts opening and closing drawers. _____

7 The cat starts crying. _____

8 Mrs. Carter gasps with surprise. _____

9 The dog growls when the man leaves. _____

## Exercise 2

Match the word in the first column (the sound) with the phrase in the second column (the situation when you might make the sound)

| | | |
|---|---|---|
| 1 _____ sneeze | a) | when you are in pain |
| 2 _____ yawn | b) | when you are surprised |
| 3 _____ cry | c) | when you are sleeping |
| 4 _____ gasp | d) | when you are tired |
| 5 _____ groan | e) | when you have a cold |
| 6 _____ snore | f) | when you are unhappy |

## Exercise 3

Decide whether these sounds are usually long or short, high or low, loud or soft.
Look at the example and then continue in the same way.

*Example: a scream   a) long   b) short   c) high   d) low*

*Answer:   a, c   A scream is usually long and high.*

| | | | | |
|---|---|---|---|---|
| 1 a click _____ _____ | a) long | b) short | c) high | d) low |
| 2 a groan _____ _____ | a) long | b) short | c) high | d) low |
| 3 a growl _____ _____ | a) long | b) short | c) high | d) low |
| 4 a ring _____ _____ | a) long | b) short | c) high | d) low |
| 5 a snore _____ _____ | a) long | b) short | c) high | d) low |
| 6 a shot _____ _____ | a) long | b) short | c) loud | d) soft |
| 7 a roar _____ _____ | a) long | b) short | c) loud | d) soft |

## Dictionary work

Decide whether these sounds are usually human, animal, or mechanical, and put an X in the right box. Do as many as you can and then check your answers in a dictionary.

| | bark | sneeze | bang | yawn | gasp | creak | crash | cry | whisper | laugh | crack | groan |
|---|---|---|---|---|---|---|---|---|---|---|---|---|
| **human** | | | | | | | | | | | | |
| **animal** | X | | | | | | | | | | | |
| **mechanical** | | | | | | | | | | | | |

## Think about

1 Can you make all the different sounds in the above exercises?
2 How many noises can you hear at the moment?
3 Why is there so much noise in modern living? What can be done to make our lives quieter?

# 3.9 Materials

## Words in context

*Read the following passage and do the exercises.*

In Great Britain, the waste material that people throw out of their houses is called **rubbish** or **refuse**. In the United States, it is callèd **trash** or **garbage**. The words may be different but the dictionary definitions are the same: stuff that is useless and not wanted. But is household waste really useless, or is there money to be made from it?

In 1971, Max Spendlove, an Amercian, came up with the idea that "there is **gold** in garbage." Spendlove was particularly interested in the amount of useful **metal** we throw away. Every day, we throw away pieces of metal that could be saved and used again. We throw away the **tin** from food cans. We throw away the **aluminum** from soft drink and beer cans. We get rid of old machines and household products that contain iron and **steel**, such as old coat hangers and cooking pots. Since Spendlove came up with his idea, many companies have found ways to remove the metals from our garbage.

Today, many people think more carefully about what they throw away, and many things are saved and used again. Each year, for example, forty-six billion **glass** bottles or jars are produced. One in fifteen of these bottles will be used again. Almost fifty percent of all aluminum cans come from recycled aluminum. Much of the **cardboard** used in supermarkets for packing food and goods comes from recycled **paper** (thirty percent of all household waste is paper). So next time you pick up a cardboard box, look inside. If the cardboard is gray, it is probably made from recycled newspaper. Who knows—maybe the one you threw out last year!

## Exercise 1

*Choose the best answer, according to the passage.*

1 In the first paragraph, how many words mean waste material?
   a) three      b) four      c) five

2 Spendlove thought that
   a) we should get gold out of garbage
   b) we should recycle old machines and household products
   c) we should save the metals in our garbage

3 Approximately how many bottles are recycled each year?
   a) three billion      b) fifteen billion      c) forty-five billion

4 Gray cardboard boxes are made from

   a) recycled cardboard
   b) recycled newspaper
   c) recycled household waste

## Exercise 2

*Which materials are these things probably made of?*

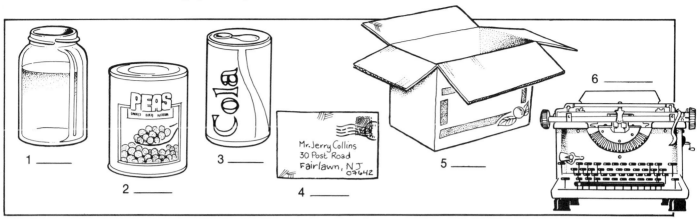

1 _____  2 _____  3 _____

4 _____  5 _____  6 _____

## Exercise 3

*Decide whether these statements are true (T) or false (F).*

1 _____ Aluminum is a very light metal.

2 _____ Cardboard burns very easily.

3 _____ Metal things contain some animal and vegetable material.

4 _____ Iron is very strong.

5 _____ Gold is very hard.

6 _____ Garbage is never worth any money.

## Dictionary work

*Which characteristics on the right can be used to describe the materials on the left? Each material may have one or two characteristics and the number of characteristics is shown. Write the appropriate letter(s) next to the materials, as in the example. Do as many as you can and then check your answers in a dictionary.*

1 wool _____ _____

2 cotton _____ _____

3 silver _____

4 silk _____ _____

5 rubber _____

6 concrete _____

7 nylon _____ _____

8 wood _____ _____

9 fur _____ _____

10 plastic _____

11 steel _____ _____

12 brick _____

13 tin _____

14 leather _____ _____

a) used a lot in making clothes

b) used a lot in building

c) comes from a plant

d) comes from an animal

e) is a metal

f) is a product of petroleum

## Think about

1 What is done in your country to save material for recycling? What more could be done?
2 Are there people in your country who make money from things that people throw away? What sorts of things?
3 Which basic materials does your country export?
4 Which building materials did people use in the past in your country? Which materials do they use today?

# 3.10 Size and shape

## Words in context

Read the following passages and do the exercises.

Object One:
It is **square**. It is 12½ inches **long** and 12½ inches **high**. It is made of cardboard and is about 1/4 of an inch **thick**. There are pcitures and words on both sides of the cardboard. At one end there is an opening. You put a **thin, round** black plastic disk into this opening. The **diameter** of the disk is 12 inches (almost the same **width** as the cardboard). There is a small hole in the center of the black plastic disk. (Now answer question 1, Exercise 1.)

Object Two:
It is often an **oblong**, box-shaped object. It is usually 5½ feet long, 28 inches **wide** and about 14 inches in **height**. It can be any color, but it is very often white. When used, the object contains water, which is about 10 inches **deep**. (Now answer question 2.)

Object Three:
It is shaped like a **triangle**. The **length** of the bottom of the triangle is usually about 16 inches. The other two sides are both about 9½ inches long. These two sides make an **angle** of about 30°. All three sides are made of **straight**, thin pieces of metal, wood or plastic. On the top of the triangle there is a small curved piece that looks like a question mark. (Now answer question 3.)

## Exercise 1

Write in the names of each of the objects described above.

1 Object One is a _____

2 Object Two is a _____

3 Object Three is a _____

## Exercise 2

*Fill the blanks with the right words or numbers.*

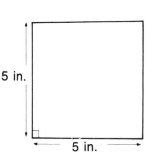

1 a) This is a _____. It has four _____ sides.

   b) It is _____ inches _____.

   c) It is also _____ inches in _____.

   d) Its area is _____ square inches.

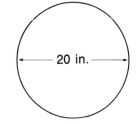

2 a) This is a circle. It is _____.

   b) It is 20 inches in _____.

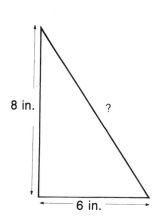

3 a) This is a _____ with an _____ of 90°.

   b) It is 8 inches in _____.

   c) The base is 6 inches _____.

   d) Its area is _____ square inches.

   e) The _____ of the other side is _____ inches.

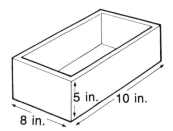

4 a) This is an _____ box.

   b) It is 5 inches _____.

   c) It is 10 inches _____.

   d) It is 8 inches _____.

## Just for fun

*Write a description of an object but do not say what it is used for.*
*Remember to describe the following:*

a) Its shape (e.g., "It is round. It is box-shaped, etc.")
b) Its size (e.g., "It is usually about 7 inches high/long/wide/deep, etc.")
c) The material it is usually made of (e.g., "It is usually made of wood/plastic, etc.")
d) Its color (e.g., "It is usually black/white/green, etc.")

Read your description to another person and see if he or she can guess what it is.

## Think about

1 How high is the highest mountain? How long is the longest river? How deep is the deepest ocean?
2 Are you good at guessing sizes? Can you guess the size of the room you are in, and the tables, chairs, and people that are near you now?
3 Can you describe a simple mathematical theorem or principle of geometry in English?

# Vocabulary review

## 3 The world around us (Units 3.6–3.10)

### 3.6 Traveling by air

book
captain
catch
check in
crew
engine
fasten
flight
flight attendant
get on
land
landing
luggage
miss
passenger
pilot
reservations desk
runway
seat belt
suitcase
take off
ticket

### 3.7 Driving a car

accelerate
brake
crash
drive
emergency brake
gear shift
headlight
over/under the speed limit
park
pass
rear-view mirror
run over
seat belt
slow down
taillight
tire
turn signal
wheel
windshield

### 3.8 Noises

bang
bark
click
crack
crash
creak
cry
gasp
groan
growl
knock
laugh
ring
roar
scream
shot
sneeze
snore
whisper
yawn

### 3.9 Materials

aluminum
brick
cardboard
concrete
cotton
fur
glass
gold
iron
leather
metal
nylon
paper
plastic
rubber
silk
silver
steel
tin
wood
wool

### 3.10 Size and shape

angle
deep
diameter
height
high
length
long
oblong
round
square
straight
thick
thin
triangle
wide
width

# Test yourself 6

Use the words from the **Vocabulary review** to help you fill the blanks in these sentences.
In some cases you have been given the last letter of the word. More than one answer may be
possible, but there is usually one best answer.

1 I think I must have a cold. I just can't stop _____g.

2 Some people take hours to pack their _____ but it only takes me a few minutes.
  I never take many clothes on vacation.

  I looked in my rearview mirror and saw that the car behind me was about to
3 _____me. Then I saw the bus coming the other way. The road was
4 just not _____ enough. There was going to be an accident.

5 The engines _____d as the plane started down the runway.
6 It went faster, then it _____ _____ and sailed into the clouds.

7 Many people have fought and killed for _____d.

8 On the way to the airport, the taxi driver tried to _____e and nothing happened.
  The taxi crashed into the car in front. Although the passenger was not hurt, she knew she
9 was going to _____ her flight.

10 This kitchen knife is made of the finest _____.

11 The three _____ of a triangle always add up to a hundred and eighty degrees.

12 "Why are you _____g, little girl?"
13 "I'm so unhappy. My dog was running across the street and it was _____
   by a car and killed."

   "What's your shirt made of? Is it polyester?"
14 "No, it's a hundred percent _____n."

15 Good morning. I'd like to _____ a flight to Cairo, please.

16 The classroom was hot and Billy was so tired that he couldn't help _____g.

17 Try and guess my _____t and weight.

18 We're moving, so we need some good strong _____d boxes.
19 They should be about 3 feet long, a foot and a half wide, and a foot and a half _____p.

20 I need to buy four new _____ for my car. Mine are no longer safe.

21 His wife complained because every night he _____ and she couldn't sleep.

22 Please call one week before your flight to confirm your _____n.

23 They were driving on a very long, empty, _____t road, when
24 suddenly for no reason the _____e died and the car wouldn't start.

25 These are special scissors that can cut through thin sheets of _____l.

79

# Index

| Word/Pronunciation | Reference |
|---|---|
| oak/oʷk/ | 3.2 |
| oblong/ˈablɔŋ/ | 3.10 |
| odd/ad/ | 2.8 |
| oil/ɔıl/ | 3.5 |
| oil well/ˈɔıl wɛl/ | 3.5 |
| old/oʷld/ | 1.1 |
| old age/ˈoʷld eʸdʒ/ | 1.1 |
| optimistic/ˈaptəˌmıstık/ | 2.10 |
| outgoing/ˈaʊtˌgoʷıŋ/ | 2.10 |
| out of one's mind/ˌaʊt əv wʌnz ˈmaınd/ | 2.8 |
| over the speed limit/ˌoʷvər ðə ˈspiʸd ˌlımıt/ | 3.7 |
| overweight/ˌoʷvərˈweʸt/ | 1.6 |
| owl/aʊl/ | 3.3 |
| palace/ˈpælıs/ | 3.1 |
| palm (a part of the hand)/pam/ | 1.7 |
| palm (a type of tree)/pam/ | 3.2 |
| paper/ˈpeʸpər/ | 3.9 |
| park n/park/ | 2.4, 3.1 |
| park v/park/ | 3.7 |
| parrot/ˈpærət/ | 3.3 |
| pass/pæs/ | 3.7 |
| passenger/ˈpæsəndʒər/ | 3.6 |
| pat/pæt/ | 1.8 |
| pay attention to/peʸ əˈtɛnʃən tu/ | 2.7 |
| peculiar/pıˌkyuʷlyər/ | 2.8 |
| peer/pıər/ | 1.5 |
| perfect/ˈpɜrfıkt/ | 1.5 |
| perfume/ˈpɜrfyuʷm/ | 2.4 |
| permed/pɜrmd/ | 1.4 |
| pessimistic/ˌpɛsəmıstık/ | 2.10 |
| petrified/ˈpɛtrəˌfaıd/ | 2.3 |
| pilot/ˈpaılət/ | 3.6 |
| pinky/ˈpıŋkiʸ/ | 1.7 |
| plain/pleʸn/ | 1.2 |
| plant/plænt/ | 3.2 |
| plastic/ˈplæstık/ | 3.9 |
| pleasant/ˈplɛzənt/ | 1.2 |
| pleased/pliʸzd/ | 2.1 |
| point/pɔınt/ | 1.8, 1.10 |
| polite/pəˈlaıt/ | 2.10 |
| pot/pat/ | 3.2 |
| pouring/ˈpɔrıŋ/ | 3.4 |
| pout/paʊt/ | 2.1 |
| power/ˈpaʊər/ | 3.5 |
| predict/prıdıkt/ | 2.7 |
| pretty/ˈprıṭiʸ/ | 1.2 |
| proud/praʊd/ | 2.9 |
| pull/pʊl/ | 1.8 |
| punch/pʌntʃ/ | 1.8 |
| punk/pʌŋk/ | 1.4 |
| push/pʊʃ/ | 1.8 |
| puzzled/ˈpʌzəld/ | 2.8 |
| rain/reʸn/ | 3.4 |
| rainstorm/ˈreʸnstɔrm/ | 3.4 |
| ranch/ræntʃ/ | 3.1 |
| rat/ræt/ | 3.3 |
| rational/ˈræʃ ənəl/ | 2.8 |
| razor/ˈreʸzər/ | 1.4 |
| realize/ˈriʸəˌlaız/ | 2.7 |
| rear-view mirror/rıər vyuʷ ˈmırər/ | 3.7 |
| reasonable/ˈriʸzənəbəl/ | 2.8 |
| relaxed/rıˈlækst/ | 2.2 |
| remember/rıˈmɛmbər/ | 2.7 |
| reptile/ˈrɛptaıl/ | 3.3 |
| reservations desk /ˌrɛzərˈveʸʃənz ˌdɛsk/ | 3.6 |
| residential/ˌrɛzəˈdɛnʃəl/ | 3.1 |
| revolting/rıˈvoʷltıŋ/ | 1.2 |
| ring/rıŋ/ | 1.8, 3.8 |
| ring finger/ˈrıŋ ˌfıŋgər/ | 1.7 |
| river/ˈrıvər/ | 3.1 |
| roar/rɔr/ | 3.8 |
| root/ruʷt/ | 3.2 |
| rose/roʷz/ | 2.4, 3.2 |
| round/raʊnd/ | 3.10 |
| rub/rʌb/ | 1.8 |
| rubber/ˈrʌbər/ | 3.9 |
| rude/ruʷd/ | 2.10 |
| run over/rʌn ˈoʷvər/ | 3.7 |
| runway/ˈrʌnweʸ/ | 3.6 |
| rural/ˈruərəl/ | 3.1 |
| ruthless/ˈruʷθlıs/ | 2.9 |
| sad/sæd/ | 2.1 |
| safe/seʸf/ | 2.3 |
| sane/seʸn/ | 2.8 |
| school/skuʷl/ | 3.1 |
| scissors/ˈsızərz/ | 1.4 |
| scratch/skrætʃ/ | 1.8 |
| scream/skriʸm/ | 3.8 |
| seagull/ˈsiʸgʌl/ | 3.3 |
| seat belt/ˈsiʸt bɛlt/ | 3.7 |
| seaweed/ˈsiʸwiʸd/ | 3.2 |
| seed/siʸd/ | 3.2 |
| self-confident/ˌsɛlf ˈkanfədənt/ | 2.10 |
| selfish/ˈsɛlfıʃ/ | 2.9 |
| sensible/ˈsɛnsəbəl/ | 2.8 |
| shake/ʃeʸk/ | 1.8 |
| shampoo/ʃæmˈpuʷ/ | 1.4 |
| share/ʃɛər/ | 2.9 |
| shark/ʃark/ | 3.3 |
| shave (off)/ʃeʸv/ | 1.4 |
| shopping mall/ˈʃapıŋ ˌmɔl/ | 3.1 |
| short/ʃɔrt/ | 1.4, 1.6 |
| shot/ʃat/ | 3.8 |
| shoulder/ˈʃoʷldər/ | 1.6 |
| shower/ˈʃaʊər/ | 3.4 |
| shy/ʃaı/ | 2.10 |
| sigh/saı/ | 2.1 |
| silk/sılk/ | 3.9 |
| silly/ˈsıliʸ/ | 2.6 |
| silver/ˈsılvər/ | 3.9 |
| sincere/sınˈsıər/ | 2.9 |
| sing/sıŋ/ | 2.1 |
| skate/skeʸt/ | 1.10 |
| skin/skın/ | 1.3, 1.6 |
| skinny/ˈskıniʸ/ | 1.6 |
| skyscraper/ˈskaıˌskreʸpər/ | 3.1 |
| slap/slæp/ | 1.8 |
| slim/slım/ | 1.6 |
| slow/sloʷ/ | 2.5 |
| slow down/ˌsloʷ ˈdaʊn/ | 3.7 |
| small/smɔl/ | 1.6 |
| smart/smart/ | 2.6 |
| smile/smaıl/ | 2.1 |
| smoggy/ˈsmagiʸ/ | 3.4 |
| snake/sneʸk/ | 3.3 |
| sneeze/sniʸz/ | 3.8 |
| snore/snɔr/ | 3.8 |
| snow/snoʷ/ | 3.4 |
| snowstorm/ˈsnoʷstɔrm/ | 3.4 |
| soft/sɔft/ | 2.4 |
| solar/ˈsoʷlər/ | 3.5 |
| solar collector/ˈsoʷlər kəˌlɛktər/ | 3.5 |
| solve/salv/ | 2.7 |
| speed limit/ˈspiʸd ˌlımıt/ | 3.7 |
| square/skwɛər/ | 3.10 |
| squeeze/skwiʸz/ | 1.8 |
| stagger/ˈstægər/ | 1.10 |
| stamp/stæmp/ | 1.10 |
| stare at/ˈstɛər ət/ | 1.5 |
| steel/stiʸl/ | 3.9 |
| stem/stɛm/ | 3.2 |
| store/stɔr/ | 3.1 |
| storm/stɔrm/ | 3.4 |
| straight/streʸt/ | 1.4, 3.10 |
| strange/streʸndʒ/ | 2.8 |
| strangle/ˈstræŋgəl/ | 1.8 |
| stream/striʸm/ | 3.1 |
| stress, under/strɛs/ | 2.2 |
| stroke/stroʷk/ | 1.8 |
| stroll/stroʷl/ | 1.10 |
| strong/strɔŋ/ | 1.6 |
| study/ˈstʌdiʸ/ | 2.7 |
| stupid/ˈstuʷpıd/ | 2.6 |
| suburb/ˈsʌbɜrb/ | 3.1 |
| suitcase/ˈsuʷtkeʸs/ | 3.6 |
| sulk/sʌlk/ | 2.1 |
| sunglasses/ˈsʌnˌglæsız/ | 1.5 |
| sunny/ˈsʌniʸ/ | 3.4 |
| sympathetic/ˌsımpəˈθɛṭık/ | 2.9 |
| tail/teʸl/ | 3.3 |
| taillight/ˈteʸl-laıt/ | 3.7 |
| take off v/teʸk ˈɔf/ | 3.6 |
| tall/tɔl/ | 1.6 |
| tap v/tæp/ | 1.8 |
| tears/tıərz/ | 2.1 |
| teenager/ˈtiʸnˌeʸdʒər/ | 1.1 |
| telescope/ˈtɛləˌskoʷp/ | 1.5 |
| tell/tɛl/ | 2.1 |
| tense/tɛns/ | 2.2 |
| terrible/ˈtɛrəbəl/ | 1.2 |
| terrified/ˈtɛrəˌfaıd/ | 2.3 |
| theater/ˈθiʸəṭər/ | 3.1 |
| thick (of hair)/θık/ | 1.4 |
| thick (of shape)/θık/ | 3.10 |
| thigh/θaı/ | 1.9 |
| thin (of hair)/θın/ | 1.4 |
| thin (of shape)/θın/ | 1.6, 3.10 |
| think about/ˈθıŋk əˌbaʊt/ | 2.7 |
| throw/θroʷ/ | 1.10 |
| thumb/θʌm/ | 1.7 |
| thunder/ˈθʌndər/ | 3.4 |
| ticket/ˈtıkıt/ | 3.6 |
| tickle/ˈtıkəl/ | 1.8 |
| tiger/ˈtaıgər/ | 3.3 |
| tin/tın/ | 3.9 |
| tiptoe/ˈtıptoʷ/ | 1.10 |
| tire n/taıər/ | 3.7 |
| toe/toʷ/ | 1.9 |
| toenail/ˈtoʷneʸl/ | 1.9 |

tolerant/'tɑlərənt/ 2.10
tongue/tʌŋ/ 1.3
tooth/tuʷθ/ 1.3
towel/'tɑʊəl/ 1.4
town/tɑʊn/ 3.1
traditional/trə'dɪʃənəl/ 2.10
tree/triʸ/ 3.2
triangle/'traɪˌæŋgəl/ 3.10
trip over/'trɪp ˌoʷvər/ 1.10
turn signal/'tɜrn ˌsɪgnəl/ 3.7
twenties/'twɛntiʸz/ 1.1
type ν/taɪp/ 1.10

ugly/'ʌgliʸ/ 1.2
unattractive/ʌnə'træktɪv/ 1.2
understand/ˌʌndər'stænd/ 2.7
under stress/ˌʌndər 'strɛs/ 2.2
under the speed limit/ 3.7
  ˌʌndər ðə 'spiʸd ˌlɪmɪt/
unhappy/'ʌn'hæpiʸ/ 2.1
unintelligent/ 2.6
  ʌnɪn'tɛlədʒənt/
unselfish/ʌn'sɛlfɪʃ/ 2.9

upset/ˌʌp'sɛt/ 2.1
urban/'ɜrbən/ 3.1

vain/veʸn/ 2.9
vase/veʸs/ 3.2

waist/weʸst/ 1.6
wander/'wɑndər/ 1.10
wash/wɑʃ/ 1.4
wasp/wɑsp/ 3.3
wave/weʸv/ 1.8
wavy/'weʸviʸ/ 1.4
weak/wiʸk/ 1.6
wedding/'wɛdɪŋ/ 2.5
weed/wiʸd/ 3.2
weird/wɪərd/ 2.8
well-built/ˌwɛl 'bɪlt/ 1.6
whale/weʸl/ 3.3
wheat/wiʸt/ 3.2
wheel/wiʸl/ 3.7
whisper/'wɪspər/ 3.8
whistle/'wɪsəl/ 2.1
wide/waɪd/ 3.10
widow/'wɪdoʷ/ 2.5

widower/'wɪdoʷər/ 2.5
width/wɪdθ/ 3.10
wife/waɪf/ 2.5
wind/wɪnd/ 3.4, 3.5
windmill/'wɪndˌmɪl/ 3.5
windshield/'wɪndʃiʸld/ 3.7
wine/waɪn/ 2.4
wing/wɪŋ/ 3.3
wink/wɪŋk/ 1.5
woman/'wʊmən/ 1.1
wonderful/'wʌndərfəl/ 1.2
wood/wʊd/ 3.9
wool/wʊl/ 3.9
work out ν/ˌwɜrk 'aʊt/ 2.7
worried/'wɜriʸd/ 2.3
wrinkle/'rɪŋkəl/ 1.3
wrist/rɪst/ 1.7

yard/yɑrd/ 3.1
yawn/yɔn/ 3.8
years old/yɪərz 'ɔld/ 1.1
young/yʌŋ/ 1.1

# Answer Key

## Unit 1.1

*Exercise 1*

1) T   2) F   3) F   4) F   5) T   6) T   7) F   8) T

*Exercise 2*

1) g   2) e   3) f   4) i   5) h   6) a   7) d   8) c   9) b

*Just for fun*

There are various possible answers to this exercise. Each student may have a different answer, depending on his or her opinion.

## Unit 1.2

*Exercise 1*

1) T   2) IK   3) F   4) T   5) IK   6) IK   7) T   8) F

*Exercise 2*

1) b   2) f   3) d   4) e   5) a   6) c

*Exercise 3*

|  | male ♂ | female ♀ | either ⚥ |
|---|---|---|---|
| attractive |  |  | X |
| beautiful |  | X |  |
| good-looking |  |  | X |
| handsome | X |  |  |
| pretty |  | X |  |
| ugly |  |  | X |

*Dictionary work*

1) −   2) +   3) −   4) +   5) +   6) +   7) +   8) −
9) +   10) −   11) −   12) +   13) −   14) −   15) +   16) −

## Unit 1.3

*Exercise 1*

1) a   2) b   3) b   4) c   5) a   6) b

*Exercise 2*

1) forehead   2) eyebrow   3) cheek   4) lips   5) mustache   6) chin   7) tongue
8) tooth   9) ear   10) eyelashes

*Exercise 3*

1) c   2) d   3) f   4) e   5) b   6) a

*Just for fun*

There are various possible answers to this exercise. Here is one possible set of answers.
1) eyes: the other three are all parts of the face around the mouth.
2) nose: the other three are all hairy parts of the face.
3) eyelid: this is the only part of the face which is not in the chin area.

4) mouth: the other parts of the face come in pairs (two cheeks, two ears, and two eyebrows).
5) forehead: the other three have sense functions (the nose smells, the ears hear, and the eyes see).
6) tooth: this is not made of skin and it is on the inside of the face, not the outside.


## Unit 1.4

*Exercise 1*

1) T   2) T   3) F   4) T   5) F   6) T   7) F   8) F   9) T   10) T

*Exercise 2*

1) f   2) c   3) b   4) a   5) e   6) d

*Exercise 3*

| color | length | quantity | type |
|-------|--------|----------|------|
| blond | short | thick | wavy |
| gray | medium length | thin | curly |

*Dictionary work*

1) d   2) c   3) b   4) a


## Unit 1.5

*Exercise 1*

1) c   2) b   3) a   4) b   5) a   6) c   7) a   8) c

*Exercise 2*

|  | blink | glare | examine | glance | stare | peer | wink | gaze |
|--|-------|-------|---------|--------|-------|------|------|------|
| to look quickly | | | | X | | | | |
| to close and open one eye quickly | | | | | | | X | |
| to look at closely | | | X | | | | | |
| to look steadily (often feeling thoughtful) | | | | | | | | X |
| to look hard and unpleasantly | | X | | | | | | |
| to look with difficulty | | | | | | X | | |
| to close and open both eyes quickly | X | | | | | | | |
| to look steadily for a long time | | | | | X | | | |

*Dictionary work*

1) f   2) e   3) g   4) a   5) d   6) b   7) c


## Test yourself 1

1) elderly   2) elegant   3) staring   4) middle-aged   5) eyelashes   6) bald
7) beard   8) cheek   9) ugly   10) contact lenses   11) baby   12) wash
13) forehead   14) eyebrow   15) handsome/attractive   16) dried   17) dark
18) binoculars   19) examine   20) teenager   21) glance   22) pretty   23) adults
24) gorgeous   25) curly/wavy


## Unit 1.6

*Exercise 1*

1) F   2) F   3) T   4) F   5) F   6) F   7) T   8) F

*Exercise 2*

1) A   2) A   3) B   4) A   5) B   6) A   7) B

*Exercise 3*

1) a   2) c   3) e   4) d   5) b

*Dictionary work*

1) I   2) O   3) O   4) I   5) O   6) O   7) I   8) I
9) I   10) I   11) O   12) O   13) I   14) I   15) O   16) O

## Unit 1.7

*Exercise 1*

1) a   2) c   3) a   4) c   5) a

*Exercise 2*

1) pinky   2) ring finger   3) middle finger   4) index finger   5) thumb   6) wrist
7) palm   8) fingernail   9) fingertip

*Exercise 3*

1) c   2) d   3) a   4) b

*Just for fun*

How many can you do?

## Unit 1.8

*Exercise 1*

1) e   2) c   3) b   4) a   5) g   6) d   7) h   8) f

*Exercise 2*

1) h   2) a   3) c   4) f   5) b   6) e   7) d   8) g

*Dictionary work*

1) h   2) j   3) g   4) b   5) m   6) o   7) a   8) k
9) n   10) d   11) e   12) i   13) c   14) l   15) f

## Unit 1.9

*Exercise 1*

1) T   2) F   3) T   4) T   5) F   6) T   7) F   8) F

*Exercise 2*

1) toe   2) toenail   3) heel   4) ankle   5) calf   6) knee   7) thigh   8) big toe

*Just for fun*

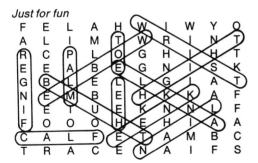

**Unit 1.10**

*Exercise 1*

1) T  2) F  3) T  4) T  5) T  6) F  7) F  8) F

*Exercise 2*

|  | stroll | wander | march | limp | hike | tiptoe | stagger | crawl |
|---|---|---|---|---|---|---|---|---|
| with each step equal |  |  | X |  |  |  |  |  |
| quietly, on your toes |  |  |  |  |  | X |  |  |
| stepping harder on one foot than the other |  |  |  | X |  |  |  |  |
| in a slow, relaxed way | X |  |  |  |  |  |  |  |
| in an unsteady way |  |  |  |  |  |  | X |  |
| in the countryside |  |  |  |  | X |  |  |  |
| on your hands and knees |  |  |  |  |  |  |  | X |
| in no particular direction |  | X |  |  |  |  |  |  |

*Exercise 3*

1) marches  2) tiptoes  3) staggers  4) wanders  5) crawls  6) strolls

*Dictionary work*

1) L  2) H  3) H  4) H  5) L  6) H  7) L  8) H
9) L  10) H  11) L  12) L  13) H  14) L  15) L

**Test yourself 2**

1) toes  2) blood  3) finger  4) overweight  5) elbow  6) wander  7) tapped
8) shoulder  9) wrist  10) gripped/held  11) stroked  12) scratching
13) tripped over  14) knee  15) slim  16) narrow  17) waved  18) crawl
19) nail  20) catch  21) hiking  22) ankle  23) thigh  24) lungs  25) clap

**Unit 2.1**

*Exercise 1*

1) to the bank  2) because it was a beautiful sunny day  3) because he looked miserable
4) in a florist's  5) rain  6) he thought he had lost some money
7) because it started to rain

*Exercise 2*
Happy: b, d, e, f    Unhappy: a, c, g, h

*Exercise 3*

Across:
2) unhappy  4) delighted  6) upset  8) miserable  9) in a good mood

Down:
1) cheerful  3) depressed  5) happy  7) sad

*Dictionary work*

1) D  2) C  3) D  4) D  5) C  6) D  7) D  8) D
9) C  10) C  11) C  12) C  13) C  14) D  15) D

**Unit 2.2**

*Exercise 1*

Type A:  a,  b,  e,  h,  k,  l,  n          Type B:  c,  d,  f,  g,  i,  j,  m

*Exercise 2*

1) b    2) d    3) a    4) e    5) c

*Exercise 3*

1) c    2) d    3) e    4) a    5) b    6) f

*Just for fun*

There are various possible answers to this exercise.


**Unit 2.3**

*Exercise 1*

1) T    2) T    3) F    4) T    5) T    6) F    7) F    8) T    9) F

*Exercise 2*

These words are similar in meaning:

| | | |
|---|---|---|
| nervous | and | worried |
| afraid | and | frightened |
| petrified | and | terrified |
| brave | and | courageous |

These words are opposite in meaning:

| | | |
|---|---|---|
| cowardly | and | brave |
| safe | and | dangerous |
| coward | and | hero |
| nervous | and | calm |

*Just for fun*

There are various possible answers to this exercise.


**Unit 2.4**

*Exercise 1*

1) c    2) b    3) b    4) b

*Exercise 2*

1) b    2) c    3) a    4) d

*Exercise 3*

1) c    2) a    3) d    4) e    5) b

*Dictionary work*

| romantic places | romantic gifts | romantic food and drink | romantic light and music |
|---|---|---|---|
| beaches | roses | champagne | moonlight |
| forests | jewelry | chocolates | candlelight |
| gardens | diamonds | cocktails | soft music |
| parks | perfume | wine | firelight |

## Unit 2.5

*Exercise 1*

1) bride   2) seventy-five   3) divorced   4) six   5) engaged
6) fiancé   7) wedding   8) wife   9) husband   10) widower

*Exercise 2*

|  | male | female |
|---|---|---|
| The person you are going out with | boyfriend | girlfriend |
| The person you are engaged to | fiancé | fiancée |
| The person on the day of their wedding | groom | bride |
| The person you are married to | husband | wife |
| The person left after the death of the husband/wife | widower | widow |

*Exercise 3*

1) c   2) b   3) e   4) a   5) f   6) d

*Just for fun*

There are various possible answers to this exercise.

### Test yourself 3

1) fell   2) crazy   3) widow   4) cared about   5) stress   6) wedding   7) bride
8) moonlight   9) annoyed   10) depressed   11) tears   12) unhappy   13) coward
14) engaged   15) terrified/afraid/frightened   16) divorced   17) worried   18) nervous
19) mood   20) attracted   21) moody   22) bad-tempered   23) brave   24) safer
25) frustrated

## Unit 2.6

*Exercise 1*

1) brilliant/intelligent   2) exercise/use   3) often   4) unintelligent/slow   5) stupid/foolish/silly   6) positive

*Exercise 2*

| intelligent (adj) | unintelligent (adj) | intelligent person (n) | unintelligent person (n) |
|---|---|---|---|
| 1 clever | 4 foolish | 7 genius | 8 idiot |
| 2 bright | 5 slow |  | 9 fool |
| 3 brilliant | 6 silly |  |  |

*Exercise 3*

1) **The Einsteins:**   a,   d,   e,   f,   h
2) **The Potatoheads:**   b,   c,   g,   i,   j

*Just for fun*

1)

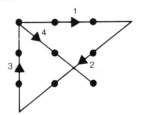

2)

(1)   (2)   (3)   (4)   (5)

(6)   (7)   (8)

3)  Tuesday

## Unit 2.7

*Exercise 1*

1) a   2) c   3) b

*Exercise 2*

1) to   2) about   3) to   4) out   5) of   6) on   7) about   8) out   9) about

*Dictionary work*

1) analysis   2) study   3) solution   4) imagination   5) memory   6) knowledge
7) concentration   8) realization   9) prediction   10) understanding

## Unit 2.8

*Exercise 1*

1) F   2) T   3) T   4) F   5) T   6) F   7) F   8) T   9) F

*Exercise 2*

1) d, g, i   2) a, b, e   3) c, f, h

*Exercise 3*

1) d   2) g   3) f   4) a   5) c   6) h   7) b   8) e

*Dictionary work*

| after too much alchohol | when you can't understand | when you are very surprised | after turning around and around |
| --- | --- | --- | --- |
| intoxicated | puzzled | astonished | giddy |
| drunk | confused | amazed | dizzy |

**Unit 2.9**

*Exercise 1*

a) 4   b) 1   c) 6   d) 5   e) 3   f) 2

*Exercise 2*

1) +   2) +   3) −   4) −   5) −   6) +   7) −   8) +
9) +   10) +   11) −   12) +

*Exercise 3*

1) e   2) b   3) g   4) f   5) d   6) c   7) h   8) a

*Dictionary work*

1) c   2) g   3) f   4) a   5) d   6) b   7) e

**Unit 2.10**

*Exercise 1*

1) A   2) A   3) A   4) B   5) A   6) A

*Exercise 2*

a) hospitable   b) tolerant   c) traditional   d) self-confident   e) polite   f) optimistic

*Exercise 3*

These words are opposite in meaning:

| | | |
|---|---|---|
| tolerant | and | narrow-minded |
| shy | and | outgoing |
| rude | and | polite |
| pessimistic | and | optimistic |
| lazy | and | hard-working |

*Just for fun*

There are various possible answers to this exercise.

***Test yourself 4***

1) rude   2) know   3) concentrate   4) dishonest   5) materialistic  6) strange
7) realized   8) foolish   9) sensible   10) idiot   11) cheating   12) solve
13) puzzled   14) optimistic   15) greedy   16) selfish   17) traditional
18) generous   19) lazy   20) stupid   21) genius   22) predict   23) clever
24) shy   25) peculiar

**Unit 3.1**

*Exercise 1*

1) T   2) F   3) T   4) F   5) T   6) F   7) T   8) F

*Exercise 2*

1) b   2) d   3) a   4) c   5) e

*Exercise 3*

1 _____ hill    __X__ mountain     7 __X__ river    _____ stream

2 _____ town    __X__ city     8 __X__ park    _____ yard

3 __X__ city    _____ business district     9 __X__ shopping mall    _____ department store

4 _____ field    __X__ countryside     10 _____ factory    __X__ industrial area

5 __X__ urban area    _____ downtown area     11 __X__ rural area    _____ farm

6 __X__ skyscraper    _____ house     12 _____ house    __X__ residential area

*Dictionary work*

1) –  2) H  3) H  4) H  5) –  6) H  7) –  8) H  9) –  10) –
11) H  12) –  13) –  14) H  15) –

## Unit 3.2

*Exercise 1*

1) b  2) b  3) c  4) b  5) a  6) b

*Exercise 2*

1) e  2) b  3) d  4) i  5) l  6) c
7) k  8) f  9) j  10) g  11) a  12) h

*Dictionary work*

1) g  2) d  3) h  4) f  5) c  6) a  7) i  8) b  9) e

## Unit 3.3

*Exercise 1*

1) F  2) T  3) F  4) F  5) T  6) F  7) F  8) F  9) T  10) T

*Exercise 2*

1) c  2) h  3) a  4) g  5) e  6) b  7) d  8) f

*Exercise 3*

1) e  2) c  3) b  4) g  5) a  6) d

*Dictionary work*

| insects | birds | fish and reptiles | mammals |
|---------|-------|-------------------|---------|
| wasp | parrot | shark | mouse |
| fly | owl | crocodile | goat |
| beetle | seagull | lizard | tiger |

**Unit 3.4**

*Exercise 1*

| | rains often | only chilly in winter | changeable | drizzles | sudden showers | smoggy | never snows | can be boiling |
|---|---|---|---|---|---|---|---|---|
| **London** | X | | X | X | X | | | |
| **Los Angeles** | | X | | | | X | X | X |

*Exercise 2*

1  X  fog  _____  mist          4  _____  raining  X  pouring

2  _____  cold  X  freezing      5  _____  breeze  X  wind

3  _____  chilly  X  cold        6  _____  snowstorm  X  blizzard

*Exercise 3*

1) cloudy, showers
2) rain
3) hot, sunny
4) windy
5) thunder, lightning, storms

*Just for fun*

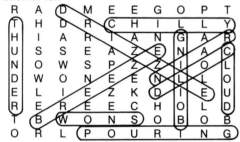

**Unit 3.5**

*Exercise 1*

1) black   2) hydroelectric power   3) oil   4) nuclear   5) gas   6) windmills
7) dam   8) nuclear

*Exercise 2*

1) a   2) j   3) b   4) c   5) f   6) e   7) h   8) d   9) g   10) i

*Just for fun*

There are various possible answers to this exercise.

**Test yourself 5**

1) whale   2) mammal   3) monkey   4) branch   5) suburbs   6) weeds
7) grass   8) ranch   9) nuclear   10) oil/coal   11) blossoms
12) skyscrapers   13) leaves   14) rats   15) countryside   16) lightning   17) snakes
18) fog   19) towns   20) shower   21) power   22) windmill   23) freezing
24) blizzard   25) cloudy

**Unit 3.6**

*Exercise 1*
1) j  2) k  3) g  4) f  5) a  6) l  7) d  8) b  9) i  10) c  11) e  12) h

*Exercise 2*
1) reservations desk  2) runway  3) crew  4) pilot  5) passenger  6) flight attendant

*Exercise 3*
1) e  2) d  3) h  4) g  5) f  6) a  7) c  8) b  9) j  10) i

*Just for fun*
There are various possible answers to this exercise.


**Unit 3.7**

*Exercise 1*
a) 8  b) 4  c) 2  d) 3  e) 7  f) 1

*Exercise 2*
1) g  2) a  3) c  4) f  5) h  6) b  7) e  8) d  9) i

*Dictionary work*
1) b  2) e  3) c  4) f  5) g  6) i  7) a  8) d  9) h


**Unit 3.8**

*Exercise 1*
1) The dog only barks for a couple of seconds so it must know the man.
4) The man unlocks the door with one click so he probably has a key to the door.
5) The man turns on the lights almost immediately so he knows where the light switch is, even in the dark.
6) He walks straight to the study and starts opening and closing drawers so he knows where the study is.

*Exercise 2*
1) e  2) d  3) f  4) b  5) a  6) c

*Exercise 3*
1) b, c  2) a, d  3) a, d  4) a, c  5) a, d  6) b, c  7) a, c

*Dictionary work*

|  | bark | sneeze | bang | yawn | gasp | creak | crash | cry | whisper | laugh | crack | groan |
|---|---|---|---|---|---|---|---|---|---|---|---|---|
| **human** |  | X |  | X | X |  |  | X | X | X |  | X |
| **animal** | X | X |  | X |  |  |  | X |  |  |  |  |
| **mechanical** |  |  | X |  |  | X | X |  |  |  | X |  |


**Unit 3.9**

*Exercise 1*
1) b  2) c  3) a  4) b

*Exercise 2*
1) glass  2) tin  3) aluminum  4) paper  5) cardboard  6) metal

*Exercise 3*

1) T   2) T   3) F   4) T   5) F   6) F

*Dictionary work*

1) a, d   2) a, c   3) e       4) a, d   5) c       6) b       7) a, f
8) b, c   9) a, d   10) f      11) b, e   12) b       13) e       14) a, d


**Unit 3.10**

*Exercise 1*

1) record album/record sleeve     2) bathtub     3) clothes hanger

*Exercise 2*

1) a) square, straight   b) 5, high   c) 5, width   d) 25
2) a) round   b) diameter
3) a) triangle, angle   b) height   c) long   d) 24   2) length, 10
4) a) oblong   b) deep   c) long   d) wide

*Just for fun*

There are various possible answers to this exercise.


***Test yourself 6***

1) sneezing   2) suitcase   3) pass       4) wide   5) roared
6) took off   7) gold   8) brake   9) miss   10) steel   11) angles   12) crying
13) run over   14) cotton   15) book   16) yawning   17) height
18) cardboard   19) deep   20) tires   21) snored   22) reservation
23) straight   24) engine   25) metal